CoolHandBrand Presents

LV. 3

JOSEPH B. ALI

Copyright © 2023 Joseph B. Ali.

All rights reserved. No part of this book may be reproduced, stored, or transmitted by any means—whether auditory, graphic, mechanical, or electronic—without written permission of both publisher and author, except in the case of brief excerpts used in critical articles and reviews. Unauthorized reproduction of any part of this work is illegal and is punishable by law.

ISBN: 979-8-88640-710-5 (sc)
ISBN: 979-8-88640-711-2 (hc)
ISBN: 979-8-88640-712-9 (e)

Because of the dynamic nature of the Internet, any web addresses or links contained in this book may have changed since publication and may no longer be valid. The views expressed in this work are solely those of the author and do not necessarily reflect the views of the publisher, and the publisher hereby disclaims any responsibility for them.

One Galleria Blvd., Suite 1900, Metairie, LA 70001
1-888-421-2397

INTRODUCTION

To be perfectly honest, I don't know why I wrote this book. In the process of making it, I found myself wondering how I could help someone who might be in one or more of the situations presented in here. Now that I have begun writing and expressing my feelings, it's a question I really don't know the answer to. I know this book will help both good and bad people become perfectionists in their attempts to do something to one another.

I'm giving away a weapon that can do both harm and good for society. I feel as though I should express myself as best I can, and writing about it will always be the best way to do it. In this book, you will learn a great deal about people. You will learn how they operate, how they think, and how to reflect on each subject.

As more information was added to this book, the distraction of not completing it became important. I hope reading this book teaches you something valuable about your life and the mysteries of what you're meant to do. I hope you learn who you want to be and what you want to do.

When you finish, there will be at least one person you will no longer want to be a part of your life. You're probably thinking of someone right now who doesn't have your best interests at heart. They remain because of the void you have in your heart. You might have no one else to turn to. Perhaps you are lonely and too lazy to find someone better.

Read this book with a grain of salt. Some of the analyses and depictions in this book are based on personal experiences and observations. Be positive, keep an open mind, and use the words as a mirror to reflect yourself and fix what you don't like. Thank you for stopping by and taking time out of your busy day to hear what I have to say. Learn through me, for me, and from me. Learn from my mistakes, hesitations, and bad choices. They might prevent you from going down the same path. I'll see you at the finish line. Let's toast to the good life. Cheers!

What Is Level 3?

Level 3 is a status of being the best! It is the base of knowledge someone achieves between perfection and continuous practice. When the student becomes the master, you reach the peak of your wisdom and skill. You reach toward a goal. You will become aware that you're gifted, and any weaknesses you inherited will be eliminated. You are a professional now. Other people seek advice from you in your area of expertise. You are patient and talented. Respect yourself and what you want out of life.

To reach that point of success, you're going to have to master a few core strategies and principles. You will survive and rise to the top of your field. Whenever you become the best at what you do and love, at least one person won't want to see you in that position. You must become aware of your surroundings and everyone who is a potential threat on a deeper, more intimate level. *Level 3* helps you develop tactical skills of the mind and keep manipulating situations from poisoning your hopes and dreams.

INTRODUCTION

Just like you, I want a life that is cut and dry—no in between, additives, or extra ingredients. I just want good old-fashioned hopes and dreams. The difference in all of us is how we go about getting it done. I chose to write a book about some experiences during my travels. I tried to obtain a car that was too fast and house that was too big. It's not that I don't deserve any of those things, but they are not necessary and never were.

Before I became successful, I enjoyed simple luxuries: going to the movies, eating at my favorite restaurants, dating, and fixing up my old schools. I started out selling candy at my high school during junior and senior year. The school was rebuilt and renamed recently, but I still remember it like it was yesterday. In the hallways—before and after class—I was making serious sales and gaining charisma from all the interactions on a daily basis.

I started to notice how people wanted me to be more social. People who never liked me would engage with me in a way that was not conducive to the way I did business. One day, everything would go smoothly, and then another day, I would get in big trouble for being in the wrong place at the wrong time. I learned many skills, including business management, which is important to running a successful entity.

I realized it wasn't what I was doing that was pissing off other students—it was the money I was generating. I was training to become an entrepreneur. After graduation, I began a brief job as a custodian. I took pride in my job as a maintenance man. I was cleaning offices and windows, and the soft steady-paying job was a safety blanket for me. On some days, we didn't do any work. We would chill in a giant makeshift broom closet. That position taught me about pride and craftsmanship in the work you do for others.

One day, as I finished cleaning a window and then mopping the outer area of a skating arena, a bird flew right into the window. I was amazed and shocked, and my boss was impressed. I didn't make a big deal because I was only doing what I was told. Working in those conditions taught me a great lesson about being in business with other people—even if I was an employee.

I was a cleaning specialist, but I wasn't just any cleaning specialist. I worked for my city. My life took a turn when I was laid off. I worked in a suburb, but thanks to that mishap, I was sent on a journey to find myself. I had to reevaluate what was important to me and what were just fluffy, materialistic things that everybody likes to show off.

After losing my job, I quickly bounced back and found a door-to-door sales job to try to replace that lost income. That job was the opposite of my maintenance job. The work was much harder. I walked at least three miles a day, from eleven until nine, knocking on doors. It was a commission-based job. I was walking down the street of an inner-city neighborhood, and it was hot. I was exhausted, and I hadn't made any sales yet.

I wondered, *Is this what I really want from my life?*

The answer immediately came to me: "No!" At that moment, I decided that I no longer wanted to take orders from anyone else or work for anyone else. After that brief decision, I came back to reality and un-paused my life. I stopped standing under the streetlight and finished crossing the street. From that moment on, the journey began. My energy and ambitions were toward nothing more than becoming my own boss.

What you're about to read is nowhere near what actually happened. I'm only giving you the end result. Some things you read in this book were the result of suffering to discover a proper solution for the matter.

I hope the knowledge of my trials and tribulations finds you in good spirits and offers you a much better perspective as to what to expect from the situation you might be going through. I love business, and I love helping others, but I do not tolerate betrayal or deceit from anyone—and neither will you. It is time to learn how to kick some royal ass. Enjoy your reading—cheers!

I used to look to the sky and wonder if someone else was thinking the same thing I was thinking in the exact same way at the exact same time. The answer is yes. Always remember that somebody—somewhere—is thinking and imagining the same thing you are. They are looking for a partner to help them along the way.

A lot of people have dreams and ambitions, but they don't want to do it alone. They might be afraid of proceeding by themselves. The art of reaching any goal can be accomplished much faster and more effectively by helping others reach their highest potential. If you are going to be the best at a craft, experience is the best teacher. Why not shorten the learning curve by meeting more people, taking more risks, and grabbing as many opportunities as possible? People are the best when it comes to honing your skills, and helping somebody can teach you something. This book offers a clean vision of how you are doing some things wrong and how you can do other things better.

★ ★ ★

"If you have no enemies inside your circle, then your enemies outside can do no harm."

"If you want to know how tall a building is going to be, look at how deep the foundation is."

"It amazes me the trouble one can start and involves himself sitting in a room quietly."

"It's good to help someone succeed above you to have a defending hand later."

"Never blink in the eye of adversity."

"The proof that something can be done is that someone else has already done it."

"The winners at a poker table are the ones laughing and telling jokes. The losers are saying, shut up and deal the cards."

"Patience and persistence have a magical effect. Before them, difficulties disappear, and obstacles vanish."

"If honesty didn't exist, it would create a fortune in the production and selling of it."

"You will always win, and you will always lose—at the exact same time."

"Anger is one letter away from danger."

"I never look at the menu. If the restaurant can't make it, I don't eat there."

"Hell is seeing the truth too late."

"Never help someone find the words for any particular subject. If you know, so should they."

"Don't come to me with your process—come to me with your progress."

"Take care of the downside, and the upside will take care of itself."

"Successful people learn how to condense time." "The only way to stay happy is to give." "Live out of profits and not out of principle."

"Money has no gray areas. Somebody loses, and somebody wins."

"You don't save yourself from drowning. Someone on stable ground pulls you up."

"I'd rather be quiet than be a hypocrite."

"A man not convinced—his will is of the same opinion still." "Do the thing you fear the most, and the death of fear is certain."

"Be sure your brain is engaged before putting your mouth in gear." "Allow yourself to have what you seek."

"For individuals, character is destiny. For organizations, culture is destiny."

"The greatest expense should be an investment into yourself. Learn how you learn, how you like, how you love, how you desire, how you find pleasure, how you feel anger, how you rest, how you play, how you lose, and how you win."

"People rarely succeed unless they have fun doing it."

"Most people learn best by the sense they love to use the most." "All knowledge is just an answer to a question."

"Christ works inside out, and the world works outside in." "Never let anyone be aware of what you know."

"To whom much is given much is required." "Nobody is going to flow you until they know you."

"If you don't want your enemy to escape, don't comment." "Never deliver verbal messages through other people." "Don't like your situation? Change your world." "Pay someone else to worry."

"If it's to be, it's up to me."

"Don't panic and don't get mad."

"Never use extra words."

"Never ask the same question twice."

"Do not apologize for future actions you haven't committed yet."

"The same energy it takes to succeed there is a person with the same energy to stop you if you are not careful."

"It's not what you wanna do—it's what you're gonna do." "You drive for show and putt for dough."

ABSENCE

Why not use what is said and done behind our backs to our advantage? Why not use the words of others to spread the message about who you are? People will say and do a lot to disrespect you, but in the end, as long as they continue to talk about you, that is all that matters. You can't control what others say and do, but you can control how you react. Like water through a pipe, if you learn how to bend the flow and redirect it, you will be able to fill a bucket. Instead of being present at every event and every showing, try going to the most important one. That's it. Only show up to people's events if you feel they will be a great asset in the end. This will demonstrate your ability to coordinate with others and show that are willing to work as a team. The message is clear that you only come out when it's important, and it tells people your time is more valuable than they realize. Only use it for wise purposes.

To gain favor of those in attendance, your presence must be felt twice as much as when you are not around. People get excited by the concept of what it would be like to hang around you. Play on that—even if you sneak in somewhere and observe how people react when you are not present. The people who talk badly in your absence should never get the chance to be seen with you. It makes you look like a hypocrite.

ABSOLUTION

Don't say, do, or consume anything or consider the information you receive until you know exactly who and what you are dealing with. The goal of absolution is to be sure of all the thoughts and data you gather. Becoming sure of the thoughts you receive on any subject matter can lead to information that you do not want to know or receive. Before the situation becomes important enough to discover facts and details, you must assure yourself that seeking this information is necessary. When you get information about anyone, especially an enemy, it should be crucial for what you are going to do once you receive it.

People are not what they seem, and neither is the situation you find yourself in. Always be aware that the information you seek will be more dramatic and revealing than any of the situations life brings you. When looking up data and information on a specific topic, it's going to bring about weaknesses. Information on anything always brings the details in the building of the present moment in which you began your research. The weaknesses and strengths of an enemy or situation are left in the past. To be sure of anything is to know more of the past than the present. An easier way to defeat anything that brings about a problem is to learn about its construction and purpose. The genetic code and construction of all are in the details of the past. You are sure of a break in your assumptions by knowing all the facts.

ACCEPTANCE

The art of acceptance is an agreement in the situations and scenarios that have been put before you. There is no alternative. What has happened is the way things are and will remain. The most you can do sometimes is just understand and be able to compromise. If you cannot compromise, move on. You can sit around and hope for things to change and not be willing to contribute to the building blocks it takes to get things done. Don't confuse it with denial because being in denial is insurance against the alternative from occurring without your foresight.

People will do things against you. So what? Situations will go bad. So what? Those around you will love or betray you. So what? The most important weapon you will ever possess is a sound mind. Letting the uncontrollable put you in a position of distrust is not healthy, and it ultimately leads to a worse situation. From now on, you should anticipate that something could go wrong. You would like to be ready for a solution. Practice breathing in and out, practice not caring, and practice laughing in the face of a tragedy. This type of behavior builds up your durability.

Accept that you might not succeed the way you want. You will succeed in the way you want. Have an even scale of doubt on both ends, and then throw that doubt out the window and prepare yourself for what is to come. You will be great, but first, you will have to accept that you will be great. Allow your presence to evolve before you.

ACCEPT THE VICTORY

The problem with people today is they need gratification in everything. The school system decides to give rewards for coming in second, third, fourth, and even fifth place. That doesn't seem fair. That's like winning with no work. What is the point of training for a victory if you are rewarded for just showing up? You can see where the confusion starts because those who are going to be victorious don't see the point in their efforts. When coming in first place, you're still dragging along those who followed with no effort. It's like a train. Those coming in second place, third place, and so on are just along for the ride. This type of atmosphere is everywhere. Do not let it affect your right to win.

When you win an argument, a battle, or another situation, not being used to an authentic victory will lead you to believe you have to continuously fight. That is not the case. Let yourself have a win every now and then. When you defeat something, throw it in the past and leave it there. Don't waste your time doing something over and over after you win. You have to look down at people, but be gracious and appreciative and let yourself be on top of whatever you win.

People these days try to make you feel like it's wrong to win. They wouldn't feel that way if they were in your position—and neither should you. Be proud of everything you gain. Spoil yourself sometimes. You work—and that's great. Let yourself shine every now and then.

ACTIONS AND TIMING

Some people will save weapons to harm you. Some people are too far gone to feel anything but pain. You could be indulging in a pleasure with them, but they will look at you viciously. Your enemies will pretend they like you. They will observe what makes you who you are and develop weapons for later. It might not hurt now, but it will in the future if you are not careful.

Pay attention to what you see in the mirror. Visualize the best version of yourself, look at how that person is built, and analyze what hurts. Determine what will make you strong in the future. Pay attention to who comes around. Every new accomplishment comes at a price. Don't let it be the reward you seek. Your goal is worth losing an unworthy ally. You will be attacked because they are trying to put a ceiling on you. They are jealous of how you are growing.

ADAPTATION

Gaining the upper hand over your life and the success of your dreams is going to be a great asset in your bag of tricks to overcome the bullshit in the way. Problem after problem, change after change, and solution after solution—trust the routine will come in this order. If you don't want to face the same issues over and over, then alter your habits each time an issue occurs. If you live near the beach, it's important to learn how to swim. After you learn how to swim, you realize the waves are becoming more aggressive. When they become too big to handle, the lifeguard has to rescue you. It might okay to be saved once because you might never enter the water again—at least not the near the beach. If you are a fisherman or a lifeguard, you must acquire the abilities to endure the terrain in which you are set.

The same thing happens with anything you are faced with. In any situation, you must use the skills presented to you. It might be less than what you are accustomed to, and you might already know things. You might know how to ride a bike, but you might not have ridden one in a long time. You might know how to fix a flat tire, and you have the talent to get on a bike and pedal to safety.

Outsmarting someone or something is no different. Adaptation is a learning ability that requires you to outsmart yourself and come up with ways to figure out a solution. From your most basic memory to the oldest thing you've ever done, think for yourself. Never forget anything you learn—and have respect for going through it the first place. Every single thing you are faced with is a learning lesson. It can be good or bad. Instead shutting off the past, save it. Learn to incorporate it in the future. After a while, if you can keep your head on straight and your mind focused, you will notice life getting a bit repetitive. Just don't let yourself get bored or be fooled by things you probably found out how to fix a long time ago.

ADDICTION

Addiction is the same as attachment, but attachment is more mental. Addiction is a physical attachment that usually stems from a chemical imbalance in the body. Drugs and other substances create addiction. The body is not able to function without the poison. Marijuana can be addictive, but it is not as addictive as other substances.

An addiction is hard to quit, especially when you need to. If you have to pass a drug test, it might be hard if you are chemically addicted to a substance. If you are addicted chemically, your body gets sick if you don't sustain the consumption of certain drugs. That doesn't go well for anyone because the body will start to have cravings.

Addiction is like a disease, yet when it really matters, people are able to quit in an instant. The threat of death can push someone to say no and begin the battle of staying sober. Adrenaline has an addiction factor to it and can be dangerous. Whatever the body craves, you must learn to control. Learn how to empower the mind when you need it most.

The influences that cause people to suddenly say no are required when it is important to control yourself.

You need to be able to control how you feel when the time is right. Practice makes perfect, and the best way to remove something from your system is to wean yourself off gently. Lower dosages, less consumption, and less importance is the best route to avoid any influence that is too much of a burden on the body.

AFFIRMATIONS, ACKNOWLEDGMENTS, AND EXPOSURE

When people are against you, they might discover something while trying to uncover the truth. Villainous behavior is when they know the truth but don't acknowledge it until others find out. These are the kind of people who do not have your best interests at heart. Anything they say or do is for their own selfish purposes.

You've been shown as much as you need to find out how these people really feel about you. Don't pretend like they care in the future. Do what you must. Stay away from everyone you can't trust. To avoid sabotaging your goals, find out something that can bail you out of trouble and then forgo presenting it to the public. The people around you are only going to wait for an opportunity to strike again and do something worse.

When you find something out about someone, present the information to the right sources to bail them out—even after holding it for a while. Always be the helping hand for those you care about. A case will always develop where it's you against the people. Make sure at least one person has your back and knows the truth about you.

A FISH THAT KEEPS ITS MOUTH CLOSED NEVER GETS CAUGHT

Shut the fuck up! That should be on your mind 24/7 when engaging with anyone. It doesn't matter where it is—school, work, home, the gym, space, the ocean—shut up! Leave the small talk for small walks. If someone says they bought a new pair of shoes, don't say, "Oh, I got that pair" or "I have those in a different color." Shut up. Nobody asked for your opinion.

Criticism can be disguised as a comparison. You are diminishing a person's accomplishment by saying, "Been there, done that. I am better than you." Don't do that. Just say "good for you," "okay," or nothing.

If someone says, "I want that car" or "I just got my new car," congratulate that person and leave it alone. Don't mention anything about what you have. Unless what you say is going to save time and energy for the individual, it is best leave the whole subject alone. Do not be afraid of the awkward silence. Not having anything to say around someone you know is an okay thing. A lot of people will say, "But Joe standing there quietly for too long is weird." My response is "How do you figure?" If you chose to be around that person, then being a little extra quiet should be okay. It is that person's company you are there for in the first place right. They can provide a learning or entertaining experience.

AIM FOR THE WIN—AND LOOK FOR THE LOSS

The only thing worse than a sore loser is a sore winner. Be on guard for those who boast about their victories. Be especially on guard in the victories you claim over people. They can appear to be pleasant and calm but possess resentment and choose to cause you harm.

When you win at something, it should come as no surprise. It should come as a simple notion that you are on the right course. No matter how hard the crowd roars, how loud the atmosphere gets, or how much energy you receive from a victory, do not care about people's attention. The only time you should clench your fist and raise it in victory is when you overcome a situation pertaining to yourself. You can tell what people think of you by the way they applaud your victory.

Those who want to see you lose will be mad, and those want to see you win will be happy. Those who want to take your victory from you will watch from a distance with great envy and pride. They may have the sweetest attitude toward you, but they want to take your rewards from you. They question how you achieved the victory and what you will do after the victory. Never reveal how you won a battle. If you are interviewed after a game, just agree with what people say and smile for the camera. They don't need to know your techniques. Keep your strategies hidden from the other team until the last minute. Your attitude toward a win or a loss should be a complete mystery.

A GOOD SALESMAN IS A GREAT PSYCHOLOGIST

Every animal has respect for predators. Do you know why? Predators know what it takes to survive. Predators prey on things that have minds of their own. Herbivores eat plants. You only need information on that which is stationary. Something doesn't move the plant, and the only thing you need to do is have the knowledge of what will make you sick or kill you.

Carnivores have the skills of a different caliber. Though fewer in number, they possess far superior skills. Their prey has the ability to think and survive. They must know what to prey on and know how their prey thinks and reacts when approached.

In order to be successful, you have outsmart and outmaneuver your prey. To prevent escape and failure, it is best to predict the next moves of your prey. In business and your personal life, if you know where a person is going to be, they have no chance to reject your offer. The best way to know where someone is going to be is to have experience about what they will do and say at any given time—or least have a good clue.

Psychology suggests knowing the mind is knowing the person. You should study your field of expertise and the mind it takes to complete the required tasks. Whether you are a doctor, a car salesman, a counselor, or a teacher, you should know how your customers feel and think. They will learn different information from you and will react during the time you spend with them.

A PROBLEM WITH A SOLUTION IS NO LONGER A PROBLEM— IT'S A RESOLVABLE ISSUE

Always appreciate a problem when you receive it. It might be hard to say or understand. Every problem you face has a solution. The solution might not be something you want to face or do, but it will bring your troubles to an end. Problems are just problems. When everyone stops having problems, all the wonderful solutions will cease to exist. The natural remedies of the world will fall to the wayside and leave us with a sense of perfection. That is as false as the day we discovered the limits to our personal freedom.

Problems are nothing more than issues. You start by breaking down what's wrong, what is right, what's good, and what's bad about the problem. Problems can be a good thing. When you find a solution to a problem, it is a lesson in itself. Losing your car keys and then finding them in a couch might lead you to discovering the remote to the TV. Everything is a reflection. It could be the keys to an expensive car or a yacht. It depends on your perspective, but it will always be relative to the other mysteries you stumble over in life.

A GOAL CAN GO RIGHT OR WRONG

A primitive technique is helpful when you lose sight of how to organize what is important to you. Break it down like a fraction. On both sides of the fence, think of ways things can go right or wrong for you. Depending on the situation, you can focus on either one.

It's important to know the weaknesses of your foundation because that area will be attacked the most. It doesn't have to happen in one day. Over the course of a week or so, come up with twenty ways things can go right for you. Then come up with twenty ways things can go wrong for you. You will find that you are not as prepared as you thought you were.

Developing twenty ways to succeed and fail often brings out your creativity. You start thinking outside the box. When a project has been finished, you start thinking of all the ways things can go wrong. Making lists puts you in control of any problems. If you can determine the problem before it starts, you can fix things earlier. A list of things you can do to fix, upgrade, or alter expected turbulence with keep you on the defensive. Knowing how a problem will strike before it gives you problems will save significant time. The odds of defeat or failure drop.

ACTIONS COMMITTED ARE MENTAL CHECKS, STAMPS, AND DEPOSITS COLLECTED IN THE MIND

Imagine having two buckets: one on your left shoulder and one on your right shoulder. Every time you do something good or bad, a penny is dropped into the bucket that corresponds to your actions. Judging by your deeds for the day, how many can say they are leaning in the right direction?

In the mind of every individual is a safety deposit box of emotions. Everything we do leaves an emotional deposit. The things we do have a form of consciousness behind them. A prime example would be helping others. Perhaps someone on the side of the road is asking for money. It's not the size of the gift, but the thought behind it.

Imagine that you are in a boardroom, and someone walks in late. If you allow them to do it once, others will view it as being okay. If you let that person get away with an act that was not positive, your employees and coworkers have witnessed a negative act. A deposit on the negative side has occurred.

If this happens the next day with someone else, another deposit has been made on the negative side. Everyone is more than likely going to take advantage of you because you haven't gone to the source of the issue and put an end to it. With so much negativity building up, it won't be long before more and more people begin taking advantage of you. In order to prevent this, you must stop it at the beginning. Post a challenge that anyone who is late will have to complete a certain task in front of the others. Maybe even present the data you planned to present in front of everyone to keep the positivity flowing and maintain order in your personal, business, and social life. Never let people repeatedly take advantage of you—and always keep up the positive actions.

ALWAYS TRY TO SEE YOUR OPPONENT'S CARDS

Everyone you know has an ulterior motive or an alter ego. If they could get exactly what they wanted, it could be good or bad, they'd still do it. In a card game, people have things in their arsenal that would give them an advantage in any situation. If you told somebody you were going to pick them up—but you knew you were not going to—they have to get a ride home from somebody else. That would be a card they pulled to help themselves out.

If they have some dirt on you and are going to expose it, that is a card they are going to pull on you. In addition to having a backup plan or an alternate strategy, the timing of when you expose someone can be just as damaging as the information you release. Spilling someone's important information is called "pulling their card" or "pulling your card."

Always imagine yourself at a table with everyone you meet. At the table, they have a set of cards. Behinds those cards can be various bits of information and actions that can help you or hurt you. Your task is to know at all times what they have and what they are going to do. There is nothing wrong with this. If people have an advantage over you, they are going to try to use it through kindness or brute force.

ALWAYS BRING SOMETHING TO THE TABLE

If you bring something to the table, you will always get fed. If all you do is freeload, you will not be fed. It's that simple. Always bring something to the table—even if it's a small portion. You never want to be the oddball when it comes to how the team eats. Always be the one who offers something to benefit the group. When people learn they can depend on you, they will open up to you and offer more.

The alpha always gets the bigger portion because he is the alpha. Without him, the entire group will fail. As long that person is in charge and healthy, they can supply the necessities for everyone else. If you give a gentle touch at the wrong time, people will see you as a pushover. If you are too aggressive, people will think you are a tyrant. There needs to be a balance between how you treat people and how you receive their actions.

Be the kind of person who everyone trusts—but knows not to mess with. A steady person will be trusted more than someone who is not. Know where you are going at all times.

A METHOD TO THE MADNESS

Problems are nothing more than unsolved riddles. Don't get caught in a farce that attacks you and manipulates your problems. Every issue you face has a solution—even if the solution is to give up. In most cases, that will present itself as an easier option, but the fighter must seek a way out. Each problem has a mechanism it survives on.

Use the terms *who, what, where, when, why,* and *how* for every puzzle in life. Don't just look at the day's work and say you did a great job. In rough times, you need to understand where problems come from. The best problems are the ones that prevent success because there is a window of opportunity. Seek positive ways to solve your problems. Go back to the beginning and change it. Aim for the root when attacking something.

When you have figured out how to solve a problem, it sometimes spreads to other households or friendships. Have no fear in your endeavors. You will triumph. Victory is the only absolute assurance. Don't get stressed out. Solving your problem might take years—but don't look back. If you need some rest, step back and come at your dilemma with a fresh face and a sound mind. Always be calm in the midst of adversity.

ANALYZE WHAT THEY DO TO YOU BEFORE THE RESULTS

Right before your grand discovery, people tend to demonstrate their motives. It could be a combination to a safe, codes to a vault, or the score of a football game. When you are going to receive any type of data, you need to progress forward and observe everybody around you.

The ability to advance brings information. It could be the expansion of your abilities, your company, your income, or your territory. Watch how people act before and after you find out something. They tend to show you whether they want you to know in the first place.

Don't be surprised at how people treat you before and after you learn something they already knew. It might give you an advantage in life. Beware of people who change their behavior when they don't know everything about you. Just because someone in your circle is suddenly nice, that doesn't mean it's from the kindness of their heart. They might want to get closer to you to discover what you know.

Do not be too quick to divulge all of your secrets. When people know everything there is to know about you, they tend to move on or not concern themselves with you so much. It really is okay to not tell anyone anything. The less people know about you, the less you have to worry about who is keeping track of you.

AND THIS TOO SHALL PASS

What does not kill you will always make you stronger. Let all the bad things and misfortunes go. Assume responsibility—no matter what—and move on. Nothing is not worth overcoming. Be strong and look for a solution. Try to observe yourself outside of your body. Look at a victory or a loss from an outside perspective. Embrace the change. It might cause you to enjoy the ride. Like water under a bridge, it's over before it began. Let things roll off your back.

Your skin is supposed to be made of lead. Don't pretend something fazes you in the first place. Don't look in the rearview mirror unless something is coming up behind you. Never look back—what is the point? The moment you look back is the moment you take your eyes off the road. An accident might occur. Don't get angry. Let it go from start to finish. You must expect snakes to be around at some point in your life. Even if everybody around is trustworthy, the environment, situation, or scenario won't always be.

ANTICIPATION

The art of anticipation is to expect or make a prediction and be there before it happens. You will know where the rat will look first to find the cheese and know when the enemy will attack. You have to visualize the person in front of you. What are they doing at this moment? How are they doing it? Why are they doing it? What will it mean for them to accomplish their goal.

In order to be in the room and not be present, you must know everyone's mind-set. This can be done for events, military purposes, or by trying to figure out what comes next. When you anticipate someone's next move, you are trying to stay one step ahead. It's a small piece of the bigger picture. To know the next move is to chip away at the master plan. Once you obtain this information, it is much easier to figure out the plot.

Discovering the plot of movies makes you aware of what is likely to happen. In the movies, once you know the recipe for the climax, it's all over. Once you figure out the plot, you can find ways to alter what you dislike. Never reveal what you know when you discover it. Instead of telling people what will happen, manipulate them. People only have one goal in mind: making themselves happy. All other selfish ambitions are irrelevant. To redirect this scenario, figure out the plot and change the situation without knowing the script.

ANYTHING WORTH DOING IS WORTH DOING IN EXCESS

Think of that statement in terms of what it takes to make you happy. You should really base the statement around success and what you do for others. We are not talking about doing drugs or exercising. We are talking about what you contribute to the positive outcomes in your life and what you do for others.

When all is said and done, you were a thoughtful person who did plenty for others. Picture your deeds as a pillow. When life throws you backward, don't you want to have something that will catch you? Many different things come to mind like a pile of money, people who love you, a cloud of positive energy, or a pillow of positive energy.

Most of the time, you can accomplish more through others. That is the best way to multiply your deeds. Your path is a reflection of how you think about yourself. The gestures and deeds you perform in the name of others will always multiply what you stand for tenfold.

Working out and being healthy in excess is good, and you are not overdoing it. When you can change others' lives to benefit them, it will greatly benefit you. If you teach ten people how to drive, that is ten people who might be able to come and get you in time of need. That's ten ways to reach a destination. That's ten ways to find information about the roads and their safety around you. Those are ten points of diagnostics about a certain vehicle you might be interested in. Do everything you love in excess for yourself and for others.

APPREHENSION

Apprehension is the anxiety or fear that something bad or unpleasant will happen. Have you ever been apprehensive toward someone or something? Have you ever thought something bad was about to happen? Have you ever wondered what would happen next? Those thoughts and feelings are a heightened state of mind.

To control anxiety is to control your emotions. To control your emotions is to ask yourself the question about what got you so stressed. If something is going to go your way, that is a good thing. If it is not going to go your way, forget it. If your gut is telling you that something you don't approve of is getting ready to happen, what would you do about it?

If you saw a piano that was about to be released over your head, what would you do? Where is the danger is coming from? What if you didn't see it? What if you knew something wasn't right but couldn't figure it out? How would you adjust to the dangers around you? How would you fix the problems?

In general, people are apprehensive about the way they feel toward others. Most of the time, they will not demonstrate it because keeping your head down when you disagree with something is safer. It's up to you to speak up or keep things to yourself. When you have a chance to make a difference, that is all it takes to change things around for yourself and others.

APOLOGIES

A lot of people will kick you when you're down, but they might not be clearly informed. Some people only do it to follow the herd. If you're verbally or mentally assaulted, and apologizes the next day, he or she is following the herd. They didn't mean the attack, and they didn't mean the apology.

If someone who doesn't know all the facts attacks you and apologizes the next day, you can accept it as genuine. It all depends on the timing of things. A quick sorry is meant to slight you, but the same apology done quickly will keep the relationship intact. It all depends on the person and why they are apologizing to you.

Everybody is not out to get you. Some people will try to save face by blaming you and others. Be careful when addressing and being addressed by people. Misunderstandings might lead to misfortune.

ARROGANCE

Arrogance is an attitude of superiority manifested in an overbearing manner or making presumptuous claims or assumptions. Everyone suffers from arrogance. You felt a certain way before you purchased this book, and after reading it, you will never look at anything the same way. This book was written with a purpose.

Arrogance can be used against you in the worst way. It will always backfire. You can play with someone's emotions, but the ego and arrogance are the epicenters of this behavior. You can easily outsmart an arrogant person. They cannot see the unrighteous behavior being emitted by their actions and presence.

When someone steals something, it is arrogant of that person to believe they have a right to take it in the first place. When someone commits acts of treachery or deception, it is arrogant to be okay with the behavior. Arrogant people are extremely predictable because they always go after something that will spread their name and what they think gives them more power. You can play on people like that to open doors or close them for you. They can set meetings up that you seek or bring in people you might need at a later date. It all depends on how they are used.

Most of the time, arrogant people crave attention. They perform in front people by doing dumb shit. In business, you can guarantee somebody will witness what they do to seek gratification. The best way to stop those people is to cut them off from you and your assets. They only want to be seen and known for things they don't deserve.

Arrogant people haven't worked nearly as hard as they should have, and they can be figured out easily once you notice their weaknesses. Mimicking them is a start to breaking down the walls they put in place for themselves.

ARROGANCE, ATTITUDE, EGO, ENVY, AND JEALOUSY

Do you know what all five of these have in common? Everything. They are the same thing. The only thing that separates them is timing and tempo. At a certain point, corrupt team members might take your ambitions the wrong way. These emotions will begin to manifest in people and corrode those who are close to you.

Developing toxic relationships, arrogance is dangerous. It gives a sense of entitlement to the tainted. Arrogance will always be the ultimate bringer of death and dismay. It's a sophisticated term for pride. Arrogance is not a problem by itself, but in a position of power, you are left with a mixture of trouble and struggle.

Arrogant people only respond to force. You do not want to have to constantly use force to communicate. An arrogant person is on a path of destruction. You'd be a fool to stand in the way of someone who cannot be reached. Attitude is more sensitive. It can be manipulated for good or bad. It all depends on how someone feels toward you, themselves, others, the mission, and life in general.

Be careful not to harm someone's feelings while directing them to a better way of living. Ego is half of an arrogant person. Ego is what someone wants for themselves. It can be the driving force for doing something positive. For women, ego can mean obtaining a man who belongs to someone else. By becoming his friend, she works to steal his heart.

The ego can be the driving component for thievery and mischievous behavior. It all depends on the motive of the person with a large ego. Jealousy is saying, "I wish I had what you have." Envy is saying, "You don't deserve what you have, and I want it."

Jealousy and envy are extremely dangerous. They both cause betrayal. Jealous is healthy and motivates you to do better most of the time. Envy is the primary reason behind someone trying to destroy you, what you have built, or your family. A person who is jealous of you will let you know it verbally, and a person who is envious will let you know it physically. Watch for the signs and learn the differences.

If you meet someone for a board meeting or a sports tournament, within a few seconds, you will know whether that person is on your side or is out to hurt you. When you shake someone's hand, it is time to read that person. The energy and vibes you get determine your next move with these people.

A deceptive grin is only 20 percent of how a person really feels. Watch how someone reacts to you and the way they carry themselves in their interactions with you and others.

ASSESSMENT

Everything happens for a reason. However, that doesn't mean you can't control the outcome. It is not impossible to prevent the beginning of a problem. Look at the bigger picture of your situation. If you didn't do anything to provoke a bad situation, it is time to kick someone to the curb.

Being a winner doesn't mean winning every conflict and gaining all the glory. It could mean letting people gain the higher ground on you and knocking them down later. There may be a few things you need to fix when you look in the mirror. Honesty is the most important thing when looking inward. If you are a loser, change yourself to a winner. Write down what's wrong. Write down what's right. Like a cure for poison, assessment is the first step to figuring out how to fix whatever is wrong.

If you are bitten by a snake, don't use scorpion antivenom. You use snake antivenom! Assessment involves evaluation. Use evaluation to solve the riddle of what you don't agree with in your life and provide a specific solution for what is going on.

ATTACHMENT

Do get too connected to people you can't let go of later. Don't get caught up with an event, product, or substance you can't let go of later. The worst troubles come from attachment to something. Even if what you have is stolen from you, don't let it prevent you from creating a better situation for yourself. That includes ideas for creating things.

You can avoid having things you love and cherish being stripped from you if you avoid telling someone you care. Once people realize you care about something, the trouble starts. Attachment is the sense of not being capable of letting something go. That is dangerous because it may be a danger to you. Have you ever wondered why people become attached to each other emotionally? They cannot support themselves and must get that nourishment from outside sources.

People may not be able to let go, which is unhealthy in life. Being separated from the things you love is a strength you should develop on your own. Separate yourself for a while—and see how you feel. It can be animals, cars, houses, money, or anything else. Watch how it makes you feel. Don't abuse yourself by taking away something. However, placing certain items out of reach or using passwords can help you become independent.

ATTENTION SEEKERS

Everyone seeks attention seeker—and don't let them tell you otherwise. We all want to be recognized and appreciated by the ones we look up to and adore. There are two things humans can't do without: happiness and attention. Most of the time, men go after these things for women and vice versa. It gets dangerous when people who don't deserve attention start to use sabotage and thievery.

From the bright lights of a big city to a hole in the wall, people will do anything to appear as if they have it all figured out. In actuality, they really don't—and it couldn't be any further from the truth. Anybody who tells you they don't want the attention of others is not telling the truth. Watch them around other people.

Everyone wants a little attention, and not admitting that is false. Another thing to avoid is becoming a public figure. If you choose not to be around people, do not give them ammunition to use against you in the future. People are a trip and a half. They use anything they can get their hands on. You're only adding fuel to the fire by paying attention to people. Let it all go.

Avoid those who need the approval of others. That's what it comes down to. They seek the approval of others. They come in all shapes and sizes. They come from all walks of life and both ends of the spectrum. Fame is an evil all by itself, and if sacrificing who you are is what is needed to obtain it, then avoid fame.

Worrying about what others think is not worth your peace of mind. Fuck 'em. If you continue being the best you, somebody will notice. Everything we do comes from the need to be noticed. If you didn't care about the attention of others, you wouldn't have anything people deem worthy of respect and approval. There would be no cars, clothes, homes, or boats. You would only buy the necessities. Don't fool yourself into thinking you don't want the attention of someone—because you do. Admit it to yourself. Ask for the attention of those you want it from. Having the attention of the right people should put you in the position to do much better for yourself and contribute great things to society and your community.

Watch how people get the attention of others. Who do they seek attention from in the first place? You always want attention from people who make you nervous, intimidate you, or make you uncomfortable. These individuals will make you reevaluate yourself and grow.

ATTRACTION

Attraction is the action or power of evoking interest or pleasure from someone or something. We've all experienced what it means to feel for someone or something. At a young age, we begin to notice how we feel and what makes us feel certain ways.

A lot of people say sexual attraction is an element they were born with. In reality, it is a learned behavior through genetics, parenting, general likes and dislikes, and commonalities. We should strive to identify the natural causes to what we are attracted to. Being attracted to someone or something should be identified with what we have going on in our lives and who we are as people. The ability to relate to one another determines whether a bond will be cohesive, especially when it comes to people and relationships.

We are attracted to certain items and materials. That is completely up to you. What you are attracted to reflects what you like and dislike in yourself. A car reflects who we are. Some people will be attracted to a truck, and that doesn't make them any less interesting. It just means they like trucks. Trucks are powerful and are used for utility. Maybe contributing to society is what you offer.

A toy is purchased for amusement. Your likes and dislikes will change over time. This will cause many experiences. Don't allow other people to participate in what you are attracted to. The results can be fatal, which is what happens when you like someone or something that is bad for you. Observe your likes and dislikes and learn to recognize them.

AUDIBLES, INTERCEPTIONS, AND FUMBLES

In the game of football, the goal is to score a touchdown. It can be easy or hard, depending on how you look at the field of opportunity, the way you view your opponents, and the way you handle them. The first thing you do is call a play and approach the line of scrimmage. You only have a certain amount of time to snap the ball. During this time, you have the opportunity to observe the defense. If you don't like what you see, you call an audible. An audible is a change in the formation. The quarterback can change the play.

You don't always have to change your formation. You can change the jobs of the players instead of making them move. Instead of changing everyone around, you can signal that the ball will be thrown. Your opponent can't tell what you are going to do if nobody moves.

It reflects what you see on the battlefield. If it looks like your opponent is aware of your movements and is lined up to stop you, make an adjustment. If you must change your formation, do so in a way that will be difficult to read and prepare for. This could mean changing your schedule or the location of an event.

You may stage something that isn't real. Make a purchase over the phone or online instead of in person. Every move you make doesn't have to be obvious. It can provide a multitude of details. Interceptions and fumbles occur when you are not prepared for what is going to happen.

In an interception, the ball is caught by the defense before it reaches the target on offense. In a fumble, the offense drops the ball. There may be a scramble to recover the ball by the offense and defense. If the defense recovers the ball, it is a turnover. The key to victory is to avoid as many turnovers as possible and continue to gain yards.

Continue to make accomplishments—no matter how big or small. The key to victory on defense is causing as many turnovers as possible. The enemy should have an extremely hard time gaining ground over you. What you see on offense and defense indicates the moves your opponent is going to make. Having a backup plan leads to success.

AWARENESS

This is the knowledge of a situation, a perception, or a concern about a situation or development. Pay attention to everything around you. Awareness is knowing what is going on around you. It involves the senses and being aware of what is going on around you.

It doesn't take a genius to understand when something is good or bad for you. Most people are aware of small things like looking both ways when crossing the street or keeping track of the oven. Awareness is used in crowds. This is another case of being mindful. Always pay attention to the people around you. Be aware of people intellectually and know what they can do to hurt you before they do it.

When you create things, take a step back and ask yourself how things could go wrong. Even though you might not foresee all the dangers, you can catch the majority of issues before they occur. Holes in your armor might exist. Apply a little stress to find them.

BACKSCRATCHER OR BACKSTABBER

The backscratcher is someone who is willing to help before receiving help. To get further than average, you want to put in the effort to help others before you get help for yourself. This builds your reputation and comforts other people. Be willing to take the back seat for a while, aid someone in need, and lend a helping hand.

The ones who will go with you might not be as appealing as you thought. Sometimes the oddest person you know might be the one you want to join. People come in all shapes and sizes, and so does the will to be on your team. Screen everyone who claims to want to support you, but do not be surprised by everybody who makes it to your team.

It could be a male or female. They come in all forms. Not everyone is willing to sacrifice what you are willing to sacrifice to move to the next stage in life. The rule of thumb is to trust no one. If you happen to let someone join your cause, be careful of backstabbers. People who pose as help may want to sabotage you or steal what you have built. A good way to catch a backstabber is to check his or her background with previous friends and associates.

Backstabbers will stab other backstabbers in the back. This is known as double-crossing. A double-cross will always involve two people: one you can see and one you can't. The double-cross will come from the one you can't see. He or she has the upper hand. When the double-cross is made, it will be betray the person you let around once their task with you is completed. Both of you will be let down.

BAIT

When you set out to do something important or spectacular in life, it's always going to bring about people who might not be a positive influence. Success brings positive and negative people from all walks of life. The same people you grew up with, knew for years, and starved with will betray you at some point.

At least one person from your past will do you ill will and try to harm you. Perhaps it's a grudge—or maybe they are afraid of change. You must learn to spot those who should not be part of your life. Using bait might be the best way to catch anyone who is poisonous to you. There are fish in the ocean and predators that feed on the fish. If there is prey, there are predators.

To catch a fish, you must lay out some bait. Once the bait is placed, the fish you are hunting are drawn to you. The predators that hunt the fish will also be drawn to you because you are attracting so many fish. Hunting for people you like will draw out people you don't. The best way to separate good people from bad ones is to set a trap with some bait.

You should aim for the predators when drawing people out because they will be the first to harm you. Unlike fish, you have to immediately weed out those who cannot be trusted. Once they are gone, it leaves behind the people you wanted in the first place. When baiting people, set out the proper materials and give the precise location of where your enemy is and the motives they have. Place the evidence in front of them to decipher exactly what they are after.

Walking around in a bad neighborhood with a nice piece of jewelry will lead to trouble. It provides ideas to the people who are trying to take it from you. Stealing from you can mean feeding someone else's family. Understanding the mentality of those around you is best for survival. Providing options on your terms will prevent you from being taken advantage of in areas you're not prepared for.

BARRIERS

There is no such thing as barriers. There are obstacles, walls, and doors, but a barrier keeps you out. That doesn't exist. Behind every attempt to stop you is an opportunity to overcome the situation and provide a better way to handle things. The only barriers that exist are in your mind, and they cannot stop you if you don't allow it.

Assume that all is possible. Don't let the unknown put you in a place of reserved action. You never know what you are capable of until you try it. The world we live in has a limitless supply of potential that would not have been achieved unless someone said, "Yes, I can."

We have all types of technology and opportunity at our fingertips. Only the surface has been scratched. Can you imagine the concept of a computer in the old days? How much rejection do you think the creators of radios and televisions faced before making their breakthroughs? The choice is yours. You can allow people to tell you what you can and cannot do. When you set off on a path and come across a barrier, it is a good sign that you're on the right course.

If you are doing the right thing and someone wants to stop you, you might be onto something. Follow the path set out for yourself. Believe in yourself. The people around you might not believe in you. Continue your journey—no matter what—and be prepared to knock down a few walls on the way.

BE A DOCTOR TOWARD A PROBLEM

When you go to the doctor, they will try to figure out what the problem is. The patient is categorized with other patients. After observation, a prognosis is established. The probability of survival depends on how many patients fell prey to an illness. After solving the mystery of what is wrong, the doctor will record any findings for future reference to prevent the sickness from returning.

Before trying to solve the riddle of what could be wrong, they will run some tests. Learn from your mistakes and problems and prevent them from returning. Take your time to analyze the issue. After a certain age, you should not be making the same mistakes, especially financially.

BE A GIFT—NOT A CURSE

The last thing you want to do is stop yourself from being successful. Being a gift to yourself means letting the abilities you were given flourish in the way that works best for you. If charming people and putting their skills to work for you is something you are good at, continue to do that. Don't change by turning their skills against you.

If you are good at communicating with men or women, use that skill to your advantage. Some people are loners, and others work best in groups. Your task is to figure out what works best for you and put those talents to good use for you and other people. There is a reason why everyone isn't fit to lead. Don't do what everyone else tells you to do. It's like having a car when your friends don't have a car. Listening to them will send you on stupid adventures and driving in unsafe areas. With your abilities, you have to advance in life.

Eagles don't fly with sparrows. Avoid people who do not think like you. There is not enough time to be doing less than you are capable of. Make yourself happy first by doing what you love and then what you like. You can never go wrong. Otherwise, you curse the days of life by doing what you hate and dislike.

BE ANGRY AT THE RIGHT MAN FOR THE RIGHT REASON

A lot of times, an enemy will try to hide behind other people. Have patience. With patience comes clarity. It is best to wait and strike at an opportune time. Don't just jump into a fight without considering all the variables. Everything that can go wrong must be considered. Be precise, accurate, calculative, and wise in your assault. Don't waste any good blows on somebody when you can counter once and get a knockout.

People are so busy doing stupid emotional things that they don't take the time to think one step ahead. The average person doesn't think one step ahead. You must think to be unstoppable. Be smart, vigilant, and dignified in your attempts to correct the wrongs of others, especially when all is lost and you're outnumbered.

In this journey to make it to the top, haters will try to pull you down. Take heed and hold to the top—even if you have to come back for the people who helped you along the way. You're going to need a strategy to eliminate any threats. They might use information to destroy your name, reputation, and what you built. Stay attentive at all times. Keep these people away from you on the path. No one ever attacks somebody they don't know. It's always going to come from a rival, adversary, or comrade. Pay attention. Everyone has a weakness, and your enemy will exploit yours.

Make sure whoever attacks you is incapable of crippling your success. They must be destroyed completely. You will lose battles, but winning the war is important. That person moves like a puppet master. If you attack the wrong person, you're going to end up fighting a useless battle. Wait until you know exactly who the culprit is. Do some detective work and then follow the strings.

BE STILL

Things are going to arise in your life that you cannot control. Although you can't see what's on the other side of the problem, you can avoid a lot of trouble by not paying attention. Some people will attach themselves to you. In order to break that link and rid yourself of the annoyance, you must ignore them. Some people act like they need a beating, and others need you to pay attention to them and acknowledge them.

It might appear as though you're not doing anything to solve the problem, and you must be underhanded. The enemy is the enemy, and you must never trust them. Once somebody shows you bad intentions, don't trust them. They must not know what your moves are. You must continue working. Let people say and think what they want. Assume defeat if you must—but do not stop. Don't contribute to the mayhem by reacting or responding to anything or anyone who tries to draw you out with troublesome intentions. They are draining you of your spirit, happiness, and everything you've built. They are acting like a leach and drawing from you to survive. Instead of trying to stop them, let them get their fill. When they fall off, get away from them watch them starve and suffer. Do not to feed into anything you are being faced with. You have to imagine yourself in a situation where you're blind or deaf.

Stop moving and be quiet. You will see who or what is trying to harm you and bring trouble your way. Would you flop around if you were stuck in quicksand? You would be still and reach to the nearest branch. In life's predicaments, don't move. Rest for second, look around, and see what can help you. There is always a way out—you just have to look for it.

BE THOROUGH YET PATIENT WITH A DUMBASS

There are some stupid people in this world. No matter what you do for them or how easy you make it, they are just not as wise as you'd hope they would be. When planning anything with anybody, make sure you set out every detail you can think of. If something goes wrong, you can blame yourself for not being accurate.

Practice being a teacher when involving anyone in your activities. Working for you should be a learning lesson and an opportunity to advance financially. If you're going to be incorporating new people into your mix, establish some ground rules to make things as easy as possible. Don't be surprised when things go wrong. Have a plan for each individual.

If the person is in a wheelchair, keep some spare parts for the chair and access rails and ramps to help them complete what you have asked of them. Everyone has a different way of fucking things up. Thinking outside the box is good practice for learning the ins and outs. Every detail should be taken into consideration before you task anything to anyone, especially those who can't think on their own.

The new people who come on board might not perform to your requirements, and that could be because they are new, not too bright, or not fit for the job. Blame your direction and instructions—never yourself or those you work with.

BETTER IN NUMBERS

A network is going to be your greatest weapon when trying to grow your personal and business life. Every person you meet and incorporate into your circle is a potential connection to someone much higher up the food chain. Even with just a small introduction, you can cross paths with important people you need to know in the future. It doesn't matter if your friends are aware of the value in the connection—it's your awareness that counts. People can be used as doors for bigger and better things as long as you show respect to the relationship.

You are never going to be able to do anything without a network. Opportunities are like pies. With more trusted people in your circle, the better your chances of eating a bigger slice. Drop a slice of pizza in the grass, and more than one bug will share the meal. Ants have the camaraderie and assets to take on just about anything with enough time because there is a network with layers upon layers to share the portions. They might be small, but they spread the work within their networks.

BE UNPREDICTABLE

Being unpredictable is much easier than one would expect. Being predictable usually entails following rules and guidelines someone else put in place. Being unpredictable means doing whatever you feel in the moment. This might mean fooling yourself and behaving in a way that is different from your usual behavior. Breaking the rules is not always a bad thing.

To change your thought process, do something every now and then that they wouldn't expect. Strangers don't know what you are capable of, but people you know do. To avoid them misrepresenting you, do something they would not expect. Go for walk during a feud with someone. Use public transportation when you don't have to. Simple things can create a spectacle and change their thought processes toward other people.

No one can tell what your next move is, but when you establish bonds and friendships with other people, they will come to know you for your habits. To avoid someone knowing your next move, don't show them everything you are capable of. Do something they would never expect—or do something you have never done before. People will get to know you through the habits and behaviors you display around them. Change this up by showing a bit more or a bit less of what goes through your mind. Learn about the people around you—and do something they wouldn't do. This is the easiest way to be unpredictable because they no longer have the same skills you do. Use the element of surprise.

BEWARE OF THE RUSE

You may be dealing with people who want you to fail. When things begin to change, it is normal to forget details or get caught up in your work. Some people have no morals, honor, or respect for rules or guidelines. Kicking their asses is a must. A battle of deception might occur, and the victim might hand over the victory.

People you have a problem with can't always access you. This might come in the form of a ruse. They may try to trick you into thinking something is untrue or never happened. Their only mission is to trick you via treachery. It is best to postpone most of your movements and analyze what is going on. The ruse is probably the biggest challenge you're going to face. If you don't know when the conflict ended, a trick could be played on you to make you to look bad, deceive you, or reveal a weakness your enemy never knew you had. Be careful and pay attention to the games.

BEWARE OF THOSE WHO SEE YOUR POTENTIAL BEFORE YOU DO

The gravest error you can make is doubting yourself. Doubt will destroy more dreams than failure ever will. Don't leave open the opportunity for someone to steal your dreams. Imagine having a basketball coming down the center lane. As soon as you get to the rim, you stop. The ball is bouncing in place under the rim. While you stand there, the ball is available for anyone to come along and take the shot that was supposed to be yours.

Avoid self-pity, self-doubt, and self-loathing. It's not worth it to stop yourself from making yourself happy because you think what you're attempting will not work. The reason for your doubt in the first place in because you're listening to what others think and say. You prevent yourself from doing what makes you happy and allow people who don't want to see you even come close a goal seething with envy. They will be glad and joyful if you fail.

Your darkest enemy is the person who is the closest to you but does not allow you go forth and be victorious. Most of the time, your worst enemy—the one who believes you are capable and does not want to see you make it—will be the person closest to you. People who don't know you know nothing about what you can and can't do. They are random people who pass you by in life. They don't know you—and they are unaware of what you can do.

The enemies will flatten your time before a race and not warn you of an upcoming challenge. They allow danger to befall you without warning you. They believe in you, but they have no respect for your growth. They express their contempt for you and will sabotage you in the future. In the future, the pieces you need have not arrived yet. They will try to stop the parts you need and remove them from your sight. They will put people and things on your path to alter the way your opportunities will form you. They are trying to recreate you and build your future in their image.

Recognize yourself in the mirror by picturing yourself with everything you want in life—right down to your shoelaces. Your enemy will begin to remove future glories from you piece by piece. Those people might be family or friends. That's just the way it is. You will have to remove some—if not all—of the people who oppose your vision for your future.

BE WILLING TO SPEND TO ACQUIRE CUSTOMERS

It takes money to make money. You have to always be prepared to spend a little to get more. Do not forget that nothing is free. Trees create oxygen—so the idea that air is free is false. You always have to be willing to give and contribute a little. Stay cautious in all deals and enjoy getting what you put out. You can't work hard at nothing, but you can be excited to know your reward is on its way. No matter what you do, if you work at something and stay persistent, the universe will manifest what is required to bring your passion to life. When generating a current of electricity, gallons of water must be consumed. Some water will be spilled or overflow. Repairs will need to be made to the equipment. The price you pay can be small or great. If you invest in a price, going after it will be much cheaper. A price will be met to fulfill the demand for anything you want. Set aside a simple offering that you think is fair. You might not like the price, but if you decide on a reasonable sum, the demand will be less dreadful and burdensome.

BLOOD IN THE WATER

During times of success and failure, you're going to attract friends and foes. Your failures are always going to attract more people. You need to avoid publically handling any drama you find. Even if it costs you time and money, don't get into confrontations with someone who is using the public to engage you. If possible, destroy him in front of everyone—but your initial attacks should be concealed.

They want to make a spectacle of your defeat. Do not fall prey by letting a small emotional outburst turn into a frenzy on your behalf. "Blood in the water" is a term used by people when something confrontational causes a frenzy of attention. Once blood gets in the water, it is going to attract sharks and other predators. Your friends will prove who they are. They will reveal how they really feel about you. Enemies can cause trouble by attacking you. If one person tries to hurt you, somebody else will too.

Don't get caught up in the frenzy and avoid attracting the wrong crowd. Despite being involved in such matters, you could use situations like that to your advantage. If you can get the predators to prey on your enemies, it can save you the hassle of being involved in taking out that person. Once the public has been drawn to something like that, it becomes difficult to avoid.

BOASTERS ARE BURNED LIKE TOASTERS

Bragging will never lead to anything good, and it will cause many problems. Spilling information about your next move is unproductive and troublesome. Talking too much gives people an idea about what you are going to do next. Alter your plans—and don't say anything.

If you decide to build a business, a car, or a boat, you might require assistance. Don't take it as disrespect. It is a benefit that they want to proceed on your behalf. Like an elevator going up, people decide to hitch a ride to better atmospheres. They could up the price on parts or labor or change your plans. That won't happen if they can predict what you will need. Don't expose your ideas until right before the moment they are needed.

Once you say something out loud, it no longer belongs to you as an idea. Your pockets take a burn every time you write a check with your mouth. Most people will change their habits once you start to talk. It's okay to never speak unless spoken to. That is the best way to avoid complications.

Another factor to consider is price point. Someone who knows what you are up to might raise the price on a tool you need. Everyone is out to please themselves. Even when providing assistance for you, they will raise their rates. In movies, when the helicopter pilot is really needed, he raises his rates. At this point, who can you turn to? I needed a ride to pick up a device. I knew transportation options were limited and kept the same ride for the journey home. I might have been in the location for fifteen minutes. I paid the driver to wait, which meant more money to get home. I prepared myself. That's a lesson I try to keep from repeating. The best thing to do is take precautions and keep your mouth shut—no matter what. Nobody needs to know anything extra.

BODY LANGUAGE

People communicate nonverbally through conscious and unconscious gestures and movements: 60 percent is body language, 30 percent is how you say it, and 10 percent is what you actually say. When speaking to people, instead of talking to them, start communicating. Observe the way the person stands, the way they look at you, and the way they glance at things as they speak. Do they enjoy talking to you? Are they facing you when speaking?

An excellent way to observe body language is to watch a favorite program with no sound. Watch it over and over until you grasp what someone is thinking by matching their actions to their words.

Everyone has a tick to their motions. No one ever sits perfectly still, and no one ever has no expression. They usually have a sign of how they feel before saying something or doing something. It doesn't take a master to figure out certain movements. In time, you will begin to notice all the variations a person can make in thirty seconds. It takes ten seconds for someone to realize if they like you or not. The first ten seconds are the most crucial. You make a good impression. You have to give people time before assessing who they really are because you never know what kind of impression they might be trying to make.

BODY SNATCHERS

When you decide to live up to your best potential, people become a problem. Sophisticated and dangerous people can use weaponry you created to stop your growth. If you know how to use certain recipes, they will steal them. They also will steal your techniques and the people you like to cook for. They are copycats, and they copy other characters' moves. Imagine how stupid someone looks copying you. If they are willing to do that, they will try to take you out. They want to be you. You know yourself and assess what they are doing to negate your efforts, sabotage your mission, or steal from you.

Do what it is necessary to counter the situation. By copying you, that person is an unfinished product or a rush job of you. They know nothing of the struggle or hard work it took for you to get where you are today. Copying you is the best they can do, but they will quickly realize their mistakes.

CAGES

People will label and rank you according to what they think you deserve. Don't be a victim. They're going to try to box you into a corner or a cage. When you're capable of different things, people will cut you off. No one is your friend, and that gives you limits. People who care about you want you to be the best at everything.

The worst thing anyone can do is support a comfort zone that hinders your growth process. Comforting you from a struggle is fine, but comforting you to hold you in place is dangerous.

You are a cage, and you must step outside the normal version of who you are. Rattle your cage. Don't let anyone take you to a place where your mind is not fit for what you need to complete. It's not worth it to let someone become involved in your mind. That is the first cage you must conquer. The person you want to be and the success you want to have will always be higher than where you are. You can easily break the barriers and cages people have set for you. People will try to control how you react or respond. If you do not stop something, it will continue.

CALCULATE THE RISK

Many people like to dive into issues and topics they have no clue about. That is a serious mistake. Don't fall prey to not thinking about the future before you decide. The choice can be costly in the end. Assess every possible outcome before deciding to take on a new challenge.

Your enemy will not take precautions before beginning an assault. This is an opportunity to do a reversal. If somebody decides to go to war with you without doing their homework, that can be a fatal decision. Just because people don't think ahead when dealing with you doesn't mean you will make the same choice when dealing with them.

You have to see the future and have a good idea of what the outcome is going to be before you get there. When you are fully prepared for something, you will see things coming. If person reading paperwork has a problem and decides to halt the project until you fix it, it's not the end of the world. Something you never thought of might occur. Who would have thought your troubles would come from someone being unprofessional? It's best to think outside the box because problems will arrive inside your circle.

CHANGE

Change comes from the ability to adapt. The IQ of a person who is capable of change is much higher than someone who can't change. The ability to go with the flow and maneuver yourself to be able to confront someone with a different mind-set is a talent. People will try to tell you to remain the same throughout your life, but the best way to avoid conflict is to keep your ambitions to yourself. Allow yourself a window of illusion to prevent people from knowing what you are up to.

Respect change. It is a good thing. The person who knows how to change knows how to read, understand, and resolve conflict. The components that make up other people's views and dynamics are not out of reach because of your ability to understand their thought processes. How much money is in your pocket? Is it enough to do what you want? Is it enough to do what you need? Do you like the sound of change in your pocket? Is the sound of jingling keys annoying? From now on, look at the change in your pocket as an alarm to do what is necessary to create a whole dollar in your pocket. The change rumbling around in your pocket is complaining because you have not done what is required to turn those coins into another dollar. To make the money evolve, you have to adapt and understand to nature of money and its growth. In order to be quiet and undetected, be able to change yourself and the coins in your pocket. All that change doesn't amount to anything but noise and short-term possibilities, but dollars keep you quiet until it's time for expensive purchases.

CHANGE THE ROOT—AND CHANGE THE FRUIT

Most benefits and issues gained through life will have a beginning and a starting point. Start from the beginning to realize who or what the issues derive from. There are some rotten apples in this world, but they all come from trees. Like the many accomplishments and gifts received from your hard work, there will also be bad things as a result of work you do. Even if unintentional, your work will not always be received with humility and grace. A lot people will get jealous and envious because of your courage. People might hate your bravery.

Your main objective is to discover the reason why something exists in your life. Everything has a beginning and an ending. Never take for granted your access to privilege situations or underestimate a problem you can seem coming from a mile away. Change the root cause of anything you disagree with. The second you discover something you dislike, find the root source. Nine times out of ten, the weakness and creation of this development will also have a strategic blueprint to dissolve a furtherance of the problem. To change the root of anything is to change the makeup.

If an argument breaks out between two parties, and you don't know how to figure out a solution, what do you do? You come up with a solution. In order for it to be effective, you must decide where to help out. A good place to find clues is at the beginning. That is the same for any development you don't like. Find out how it was created and what is needed for this problem to survive. Most of the time, you're going to have to remove the problem by chopping down the tree and planting a new a seed. Removing friends, finding new ones, switching products, and altering forms of communication are some of the results that neutralize a problem.

CHASE YOURSELF

Many people—friends, family, and foes—think you should give up on trying to be the person you have dreamed of. The negative remarks always attack you. They tell you it can't be done. They say it cannot be achieved, it is not possible, or it can never be done. You know what you say to them? Okay—and continue moving forward.

Imagine seeing a better-looking version of yourself running alongside of you and saying, "Follow me." you would follow him or her. You love yourself enough to trust yourself. At that point, a twin appears ready to lead you. That version knows the future and can provide helpful advice to improve yourself, especially if this alternate version has everything you wanted.

A car pulls up with your friends and family, and they say, "What are you doing? Where are you going? Why haven't we heard from you? What do you think you are doing?" They can't see this alternate version of you, but as you begin to listen to them, the better version looks back, smiles, and says, "Keep going."

Will you listen to yourself or listen to other people at that point? It's the same in your life right now. Once you begin to go down a path, there will be trouble waiting for you. The least-resistant path is sometimes a detour. You have to listen to yourself at all times in unpredictable situations. Even though you can't see the finish line, you know what you have to do to achieve what you seek.

If you were to look in the mirror and the person you are looking at climbed out—after freaking out and hollering—you'd realize that person was there to help. The person I'm referring to is you. The person in the mirror is the only person who should have an opinion about your endeavors. Anyone who tries to stop you from listening to this person is someone you need to stay away from—no matter how important the relationship is.

CHEAP AND SIMPLE

The best things will not cost you a lot of money, and they will provide you with the exact means to get the job done. Trust that there is always an option to fix the problem without getting all bent out of shape and losing out on opportunities. All it takes is a little research and know-how to fix any solution. Problems come with solutions—large or small. Don't invest in trying to fix anything until you look at all the alternatives.

The best people to work with will be hard to find. They will specialize in the areas you need help in. They can make things better in price or performance. The same is true with products, places, or things. Don't spend your hard-earned money on anything you don't understand. Take your time to develop a solution. Take your time to allow people to help you. Take your time to process the problem.

One time, one of my pit bulls had a sun spot that caused it to bleed and go bald. I discovered a simple box of baking soda and a bar of soap would remove the skin issue. It took a little more time, but it was effective. I felt relieved that I was able to save my dog's life and put him at ease. The baking soda kept the dog from licking its wounds. It took a little patience, belief, and experimentation.

If you are going to reserve the funding for most things, a cheap and simple solution will require a bit of exploring and experimentation. You can always apply this philosophy toward your own performance. Look for ways to make your life and situations better with little to no resources.

CLEANLINESS

Being clean is necessary for all aspects in life. A clean person is more productive, and it helps you determine what you shouldn't have around you. Being clean feels really good, and the spirit is never better than when you're fresh and clean.

With a clean and clear mind and body, you can then focus on getting the job done. All your equipment should be clean. All your working spaces should be clean for an excellent procedure. The people you hang around should always be as clean as your area.

The wrong element might be in your presence, and you have to see what is happening without any distractions. If something goes wrong, you can spot the problem immediately. In every interaction, keep it clean. Your actions should be clean, accurate, precise, and punctual. People leave trails and clues about their intention and next moves. If your vision is not plagued by unnecessary clutter, you can easily spot what they are after. Be clear in your intentions—and go no further than what is needed. Don't mix and match people to manipulate a situation in your favor. When people become entangled, things get messy.

CLOAK AND DAGGER

The characteristics of mystery, intrigue, or espionage reflect the danger of being involved or close to people. The deception of being around the wrong people will always be a mystery because someone might have the ability to hurt you and genuinely love you with no knowledge of you. Someone might hate you and want to see nothing more than you destroyed. The cloak and dagger comes from the fact that you will never know or fully understand other people. You will never grasp the fact that someone else is out for themselves and will sacrifice you and anyone else they can get their hands on.

Furthermore, people are black holes. They have the ambition to be the best thing and be the best at it. They consume everything they can to move forward. A vacuum cleaner moves forward only by the ground it covers and the items it consumes. When the cord reaches its ultimate length, that's it. People need joy and pleasure.

When leading these people, you secure enough ground until they reach their limit. When reaching this limit, you will discover what they will do to carry on and continue eating and consuming. When a person is desperate, they either cloak themselves to remain invisible or reveal the dagger and take try to take from you. With the cloak comes the dagger. No one who is trustworthy will ever cloak themselves to the point where you don't know who they really are unless it is to protect you. Otherwise, it will be a simple display of pleasantries and other behaviors to charm you. A cloak is like a blanket that makes the person wearing it completely unseen. Watch both hands of people and be ready for the dagger that follows mysterious behavior.

COMMUNICATION

The most effective people will always get ahead. They have mastered communication. In a world of fast-paced technology, leaders are capable of close communication. It's not enough to be able to analyze and understand people. You must be able to communicate. The best communicators know how to seek, accept, and apply advice. They know how to create doors for others to assist with their knowledge, shortening the learning curve.

When speaking with people, you need to know how to hold a conversation. The best conversationalists respond, "How do you mean? Tell me more. And then what?" These key phrases will keep the conversation going. Good body language can sweep anyone you want off their feet. You will become devastating to those who have the chance to chat with you.

When speaking to people, remember that listening is more important that responding: 70 percent of communication is listening, and 30 percent is speaking. Practice makes perfect, and the most effective way to communicate with anyone is to start talking to them. When talking to someone, imagine a tennis ball going back and forth on a court. How you respond determines the effectiveness of hitting that ball back to other side. Take your time and calculate what you are going to say next. To get a head start, practice in the mirror or with someone who can rehearse rebuttals and responses.

People usually say the same things when they learn the art of speaking. Always be interested in what someone has to say. They will have a lot to say about their careers, names, likes, and dislikes. If you don't know how to continue a conversation, shift to those interests and pick up where you left off. When speaking to people, you better have an end goal. Don't speak to anyone for no reason. It doesn't matter how important they are. No one's voice is worth your peace of mind.

COMPLACENCY

There is a fine point between quitting and starting a new mission. It comes and it goes, but it's there. The visitation rights you grant complacency will be the result of how you leave this world. Complacency only comes around when you achieve it. It doesn't visit when you want to quit. It doesn't visit when you win, and it cares not for losing. It only comes after a victory. It doesn't matter how big or small, it will show itself. It whispers of stopping where you are.

You should relax, change direction, take a vacation, or do something else. Stop and enjoy the scenery. It's not important that you continue what you are doing. Give it a rest. This is the voice of complacency. It is not your friend, but the voice of complacency is sweet and friendly. It tells you all the things you want to hear. It knows how to keep you elevated, and it plays the wingman and introduces you to its cousin: *comfortability*.

They strike with devastating accuracy, and the best way to avoid a long visitation from these two is to continue moving forward. Work hard and get used to hard work. You only feel complacency when you have satisfied a basic need to achieve. The level of success is where it stays dormant and closer to the top. After a certain point, any accomplishment will become addictive. You have to break that barrier of being satisfied. If you feel satisfied with your level now, don't put yourself down. Keep moving—and don't look back.

COMPOUND THE INTEREST AND THE EFFORT

When you go to the grocery store, you gather all the items you want and choose between self-serve or regular line. In the regular line, the conveyer belt makes collecting your items much easier. This metaphor should be applied to the actions you make toward goals, people, and commitments. As you contribute more and more toward a goal, your actions should accumulate to a set of accomplishments you want to receive. Instead of money and debt, you have to pay for your items. In this metaphor, the money and debt will be reversed into money and interest. Everything you do should have an effect on your future in a positive way. Think of it as a snowball going downhill. The hardest part is reaching the crest of a mountain. Once that is achieved, it becomes easy. At some point, you should be able to sit back and collect everything you want from your actions. As you move to the front of the line, you are already on to the next goal. The credit gathered from yesterday reaches you the next day. That is why having more than one goal is important. Consistently work toward the things you want in life. It starts when you start. The sooner you begin doing positive things for yourself, the sooner the future can benefit. It's a time game that you need to start playing yesterday.

CONDITIONING

A behavioral process becomes more frequent and predictable in a given environment as a result of reinforcement. Reinforcement typically is a stimulus or reward for a desired response. Stimulus isn't always something pleasurable. Stress is a stimulant on the body and causes other chemical reactions that can damage the system. The mind is conditioned on a daily basis. It knows what to expect and what will occur when going through the routine of living. Day by day, you are used to experiencing what food will taste like, what musical instruments will sound like, and what certain pains feel like in the body. What you are conditioned to is what you will get used to. That happens through the entire process of using our senses. A breakthrough for that is to expect something different and expose yourself to different elements in life. How else do you expect to make it if have the same thoughts in your mind? It might take some getting used to. It might be painful, entertaining, or joyful, but it can change your mind. Start with your deep-rooted habits. Attack the habits that physically cause you to change an atmosphere. Habits include perpetual pleasure, eating, drinking, sleeping, and anything you enjoy too much. Change it up a little bit. Tempt yourself to go longer without doing those things. Put them off a bit longer. It's up to you to change your mind and body.

CONNECT THE DOTS

When you learn about yourself, your detective skills will grow. A lot of shit you will face has a starting point and an ending point. You will never discover this without figuring out who, what, where, when, why, and how something is going on in your life. If you keep to yourself, nine times out of ten, that shit is coming from somebody who knows you. They're aware of what you are doing. They see your potential, and the trouble begins.

If you do not leak any information and it's hard to figure you out, solving your problems will be easy. Your relationships are based on you—and not those around you. It's called keeping the grass cut low. With fewer people around, it's easier to spot something that isn't supposed to be around.

All gifts and problems you come across will be from the hands of other people. You can't do anything alone in this world, yet you can't trust everyone you meet. A person is always behind the bullshit. You should be able to figure out who is the culprit is. Do not underestimate anything that can go wrong. You can be at fault for the things you say and do. The relationships of others are important to be aware of, especially when piecing together facts about someone.

Enemies and friends don't always need a motive to participate in certain actions. Someone you are unaware of might have an issue with you. You can draw a line with people. If your delivery guy is late with the cooking supplies, your chef might have to make a veggie meal. If the somebody likes veggies in the group, did they have access to the delivery guy and prevent a certain meal from being prepared? Do they have access to the chef? How could someone sabotage something in your life? Drawing from points like this, you will be able to develop the big picture of what someone wants. A veggie meal might be a small example, but the cunning and manipulation are intelligent and problematic if applied to money deliveries. Get the picture? Draw it out from the facts and details until you see the interest for you and someone else.

CONSPIRACY

The best way to avoid a conspiracy is to avoid telling people any of your business. Once it is discovered that you want to become something greater, people don't want to see you succeed. It is not the fact that you are trying to become successful—it is the attention you might get. Some people might be sabotaged by police officers for crimes you got away with. That is understandable. You would be a criminal, and a few people might have a problem with you.

People will try to destroy your progress and take control of your creations. Trust no one completely. You have to protect the knowledge of what you want. People might gather for the benefit of preserving you and what you stand for, but more often than not, they intend to make sure you don't exist. Avoid people like the plague. Only trust them as far you need them—and stay away from the unhappy and miserable people.

CONTENDERS TO PRETENDERS

You're not pretending anything. It's more like playing the fool. A lot of times, these assholes will throw a rock and hide their hands. It is important to know exactly who the problem is and what the problem is. You have to catch them with hard evidence. They're going to continue the behavior and present themselves as not doing anything because you can't prove it.

Sinister people are full of shit and should be caught in the act. You need to be as close as possible to witness them throwing the rocks or swinging their arms. The farther you are from them, the harder it is to know exactly what they were aiming for. Narrow down the culprits, wait patiently, and pretend you don't see them winding up to throw the rock at you. When they throw it and pretend like it never happened, you wind up and throw it back with much more precision and accuracy. Their goal is to lead you into a fight that involves you using force they can overcome by exaggerating the situation into a need for more help on their end. You will be outnumbered and overpowered.

CONQUERORS

People these days always need to feel like they are in control and are standing over you. When you buy a brand-new car, something is wrong with the color. When you buy a house, something is wrong with the location. When you buy some shoes, they are not the latest edition. When you buy a bag of chips, it's not the big bag.

Everything you do will involve someone throwing some kind of jab at you. Don't even trip. It is what it is. Everything you do will be a problem for somebody—even people who are doing better than you. That is just the way life is. No matter where you are, 100 percent success is nearly impossible.

Think of it like a mountain peak. No matter how high you go, the crest is unreachable. In reality, it would be possible to reach to top of a mountain, but it's not possible from a psychological standpoint. To be 100 percent successful is to never have any problems. That is like saying that people are 100 percent healthy, and that is not the case. Your best alternative is to let them have a small victory.

Fragile people have fragile egos. If you are happy for someone, then be happy. There is no other way to put it. A little jealous is healthy, but the right mind will use what he or she endures as motivation to do better. If they have a faulty mind-set, they will get mad and envious. The closest people to you can be threats to whatever you want, and they might be jealous. Limit your attachment to one person. People come and go in life—just like the next conquest.

CONTROL

The last emotion or mental trait you want to share with anyone is your ego. Uncontrollable people don't want to control other people. Controllable people seek to control others. The people who have manners, intelligence, charisma, and the necessities to get ahead lust for control. How else can their plans be achieved? Having people who follow is a bad thing, but seeking to control others for the benefit of being their superior will never work. When you do something for yourself, someone might tell you how to carry yourself in your own adventures. If you decide to go for a jog, you might wave to a neighbor. If one of the neighbors sprays the hose at you and says it was a joke, they are trying to take control of the situation. If that neighbor suddenly runs next to you, they are taking control. They are saying, "I want to join you, and I feel as though I don't need to ask." This is a reasonable assessment because anyone who wants to properly join you in anything will approach you in a dignified and appropriate manner and ask for permission. Unless you are attractive, a celebrity, a politician, an athlete, or a business leader, why would someone feel the need to invade on your space? The person might look up to you to some degree, but would you really value a person who does what they want, when they want, and how they want? The neighbor waves and says, "Looking good!" That is a small gesture of control.

If a person offers you advice when you don't ask for it or makes a decision on your behalf, they are taking control. Other forms of control include purchasing items and offering you the one they feel you deserve: food, clothing, luxuries, or privileges. They might decide what to watch on television, where to go eat, or what to do. Choices that affect your relationship should always include compromise.

People negotiate with one another by using compromises. True care and concern come from a place of assistance. Whenever you come across anyone who has a control issue, never argue with them. Ignore their presence and move on. You don't have time to direct people. If someone tries to sabotage you, you are alerted immediately to the threat.

A neighbor might park his car in your way the next day. It might take a while before the jealousy and envy surface. If that neighbor throws a party, and the whole street is blocked, you have to ask yourself how often this person has these events. Do a full analysis of this person's mind and mental makeup by using the techniques and skills provided in this book. To thoroughly understand the intentions of this person and assert yourself, you run down the road anyway. Wave to all the attendees and check for a response from your neighbor. How they react to this behavior is an indicator of what is going on. Things can get better or worse. If they throw another party the next weekend, the individual probably doesn't want to see you coming down the street anymore. Controlling someone starts with the mind. Look for signs and indications that these people might not be good fit for you.

CONVICTION

Do your dreams and beliefs have enough conviction to become true? Will you allow yourself to believe that what you want is possible and real? Do you have what it takes to make your dreams a reality? These are the questions you need to ask yourself before stepping into situations and opportunities you believe might assist you in accomplishing your goals. If you lack the necessary ambition to carry out what is necessary, that might come back to haunt you.

The people who build skyscrapers and bridges have the conviction to establish a better way of living. It doesn't take much to want to make a difference. All you have to do is believe. That is all it takes to want to do something. Never let anyone tell you differently. In addition to wanting to make a difference, start by understanding the difference you want to make.

People are jealous of those who have the ambition and conviction to not be stopped. People may show you their true colors and want to punish you. Pain and suffering should never have the opportunity to be around you when the time is right. Those who contributed to your suffering in any way should never have the chance to be around you when everything is better. Remain steadfast in your conviction toward others who show you hatred and try to defy what you can create. They don't like you, they don't respect you, and they care nothing for you. Return the favor by acting on your conviction and removing yourself from their presence. Conviction is the source of all you have emotionally put toward your dream.

CONVINCE THE RIGHT PEOPLE

Somebody bigger and better is always going to be above you. People will be on the outskirts of your ambitions. The regulators and enforcers who uphold the boundaries are important for your mission. If they are on your side, they will show you favor in the most dependable way. Inevitably, somebody is going to try to take away what you have built by cheating. If the referee likes you, you have nothing to worry about. That will buy you the time to obtain what you need to win. If you have to go to court, but in the few months leading up to the case, you cut the judge's grass, that creates a bond between you two. In the courtroom, you are accused of something you didn't do, but the judge decides to throw out the case. The judge showed you favor because you didn't do anything. In the end, you retain your freedom. The plaintiff is shown the door for a well-calculated lie.

Sometimes things happen you can't believe, and good and bad events are possible. Always remember to be polite to everyone who crosses your path. You never know who you might need or when you might need them.

COSTUMES

Everyone wears one, but the authenticity of wearing determines whether a person is stable. A costume is a form of dress someone uses to portray an image of history or fantasy. Some people choose to be like other people. Those people are not stable and will do anything to run away from their lives. You want stable people around you— not someone who is willing to decorate themselves as someone or something they are not. It's all in the performance. Some people can pull it off, and others can't.

Those people will leave you questioning why you considered them for a role. Have you ever seen a sad clown or a blind mime? It doesn't take a genius to figure out what they are. A person must assess who they really are. Everyone does not understand who they are, but they can tell you a thing or two about yourself. Only people who understand themselves know not to speak to anyone else. When you see people pretending to be something they are not or dressing as such, just let them go. It's not your job to stop people from making mistakes. If someone chooses to be a construction worker for the day, they should bring their hard hat.

CREDENTIALS

When you see the opportunity to join a free program or attend a class, take it. Look for the ones that offer certifications or awards. These will come in handy when defending yourself against adversaries who try to falsify your intentions. No one really wants to see you succeed. You want the paperwork to show you have made steps in the right direction on your journey. Don't think of this as kissing up to the teacher. Use the teacher's voice when the class becomes aware of what you do. If they don't like you, they might try to gang up on you. Having a stack of paperwork gives you a leg up on the competition. Just as money gives you the opportunity to overpower people, the paperwork will tell people you are capable of making money in the future. You are a better investment when you can manifest paperwork that gives you the right to speak on subjects others have to work for.

Have you ever been in an argument in school when the teacher listened to the classmate with better grades? It's the same thing. A degree is the result of that argument. In adult life, a degree equates to that same lesson. Paperwork and degrees suggest you have the intelligence to work with, and it says you have the organization to complete a task and do what you are told.

DENY YOUR ACCESSIBILITY

Never feel like being alone is a problem. Think of yourself as a briefcase. Once the briefcase is open, everyone knows about it. If it were to close and begin developing activity in itself, that would be a problem. While people know what you are up to, they might decide you are not someone to hang around.

As time goes on, you will soon see that your perceived misfortune has become an opportunity for advancement. Loneliness is nothing more than unused exclusivity. No one wants to be around you in the beginning. They think it's a joke—and the dreams and aspiration you have shared with them will not come to pass.

As you begin to grow, your expectations of what you want will change—and so will your confidence in people. Your patience will become a useful weapon against those who did not believe in you at the beginning. A change will arise, and the need to be around people will grow exponentially.

The need to reopen that briefcase and see what is inside has grown. The same small leather briefcase has the interest of those who saw the inside of it and know its contents, and over time, word spread to a new set of individuals who want to feast their eyes on whatever is inside. It will be the same with you and your life. Let everyone go who doubts you and is unwilling to stick around while you create and develop new contents for your life. The same people will come running once they realize what is going on.

Make sure you avoid the relics of the past and have something worth seeing when someone takes a peek into your life.

DESTROY COMPLETELY

When discovering enemies, they have to be completely wiped out. This might sound drastic, but if the doctor finds something wrong with you, do you just want them to remove part of what's wrong or remove all of it? The same philosophy must be applied to each and every problem you face in life. Big or small, the second you notice it—get rid of it. Apply whatever force is necessary.

When you have to take people out, do it quickly and quietly. Completely remove them and all traces of them: their connections, friends, and associates. Get rid of all known sources of information to remove any threats. They could be family or friends. It doesn't mean doing bodily harm, but you must remove them from your life.

A situation might require different measures, and you must do whatever you can to find peace in your travels. You will regret leaving anything that is a threat to you. It's not safe to let germs linger. They can come back stronger. A threat is always a threat. Never turn your back on anyone who has done you wrong in the past. They will do it again if they get the chance. Wipe them out, wipe it out, and wipe it all out.

You can be the problem unless you remove yourself from the issue. Don't be biased against the facts and what they reveal because tending to yourself is crucial for survival. If an infected limb cannot be saved, remove it. There is always the ability to bring things back. Eliminate what is not necessary for you to thrive. Don't blame yourself for what happens before or after you've done what is necessary. It's a part of nature.

DEVIANCE

Departing from accepted standards, especially in social or sexual behavior, is something we are all prone to. When the going gets tough, it's time to shift behavior and focus on the negative. Many people would rather take the low road than the high road. Most people pretend it's someone else's fault when things turn bad. It is easy to do the wrong thing when no one is looking. Practically everyone has done something bad to someone else. A situation may call for drastic measures, but do absolutely everything to avoid trouble.

It's okay to stand your ground unless it means breaking the rules or disobeying the law. Everyone has a deviant streak. Only a fool thinks it is all blissful thinking. A good way to control your deviance is to focus on something constructive. Every person has two elements of existence: a good wolf and bad wolf. Each day you decide who is winning in your mind. A healthy battle includes letting less positive parts out to breathe from time to time. You want to do so much good. It all falls apart when you snap because of rage lingering in your body.

Exercise both fields of thinking by channeling that energy to positive and constructive activities. An example is going to the gun range. The gun range is a healthy way to vent your frustration, but a negative reinforcement is picturing someone you dislike. It might be a good idea in the long run. Exercise those states of mind, but keep them in check.

DISTINGUISHING AND DISTINCTION

Distinguishing is recognizing or treating someone or something as different. Distinction is the difference from one to another. It doesn't come easily, and it doesn't come cheap. When you fail to understand what you see, you see the change in behaviors that separate this from that. Being street smart brings distinction. Being book smart comes from distinguishing. They are the same. To recognize information in a book, you need to understand how to apply the knowledge you gain from reading.

Being on the streets requires intelligence to know when someone or something is not as it should be. The master of both is wise and understands that nothing remains the same for long. Things change quite often. Knowing how to handle the change in persons, places, and things—and the foresight to see the predictability in similarities—sets good apart from great. Every book requires pages and words that line up in a certain format. Every book has knowledge and wisdom from an author to define its purpose. No two books are the same. Every living organism requires nutrients, and every organism seeks to live and recreate. Chaos happens on a daily basis. Every vehicle requires fuel, and every vehicle requires maintenance. You have to know what you like or the trip to the dealership will last all day.

We have profits and debt, and we have hope and despair. The gift that humanity gave itself is experience. That experience translates into distinguishing and distinction. Distinguishing and distinction will offer a window of opportunity to survive because recognition of habits and routing will allow you to verify the similarities in everything you come across on your journey. Learn how to learn— and learn with a purpose. After a certain age, it is a good sign when the behaviors of different people appear to repeat. It is a sign you are experienced in distinguishing and the distinction of who and what you are dealing with.

DON'T BELIEVE IT

During my travels, I have realized that people will say and do anything they can to prove something is true. The most common form is betrayal. When you are true in your relationships, your intentions are genuine. Someone might decide to bring you information about someone else. If it is not a trusted source, take a look at who is delivering the message. Jealous and envious people will try to cause discord between you your friends. They want to ruin your relationships. Do not believe what you hear or see. That is the safest way to avoid trouble in your life. If you don't hear it from someone's mouth, let it go. It's not worth listening to funneled words coming from someone else. Don't listen to what you hear—but remember who talked to you. Another element of distrust to look out for is what people show you. Disregard all intel that cannot be collaborated.

DON'T CLIMB INTO BED WITH ANYONE COLD

Before you do business with someone, consider being in the presence of more people or make arrangements to understand who you're dealing with. No mistakes. Trying to make progress with a person who doesn't respect you will fail. The way they disrespect you, talk behind your back, and make fun of you is not tolerable. Be cautious at all times.

Money is not worth peace of mind. Shit talkers only produce more shit. Lies and misfortune only behold those who stay in the company of snakes. Snakes eat other snakes. How many animals eat their own kind? Piranhas don't trust their own kind.

Show love to those who are in your corner and favor them 100 percent. You can't afford to misjudge anyone. Take your time before bringing people aboard and don't hesitate to throw them over the deck. Team means team, and there is nothing worse than a person who is trying to sabotage the engine with jealousy, envy, and entitlement. These are not yes men. They tell you the truth regardless of whether you want to hear it. Know who you are dealing with at all times. Be hesitant to join forces with anyone. They might present themselves as friends but be working as spies.

DON'T GET EXCITED

Remain calm under pressure. A lot of things will go wrong, and a lot of things will go right. Don't go crazy when it happens. Develop a balance between you and the problem. Keeping calm is a great way to remain in control. Imagine arguing with someone, and they are screaming and losing their mind. If you remain calm, it makes for a better point of view because it demonstrates great confidence. It also proves the point that you are worthy of being in charge.

You are a reflection of everything you stand for. You represent what you are in charge of—even if it means nothing more than being associated with something. The calmer you are, and the more relaxed your demeanor, the more you look like the boss you are attempting to become. In harsh conditions, most people don't falter or panic. They use the tools and resources at their disposal to solve the issue.

Losing your temper is not beneficial 99 percent of the time. Be careful, be smart, and be prepared. You have to preserve your way of life. Stay calm—and you will recognize when the time is right to attack. An attack can be accurate and precise. Remain calm and seize the right moment to hit the target. That target will never be reached if the sniper loses it during the aiming process. When lining up the target, stay calm. No one can tell what you are planning or thinking if you always have the same attitude.

DO NOT STRIKE UNLESS IT HURTS

A lot of people are quick to relinquish information and point out something that will be damaging to the next person. You are not going to do that. Study why a person has a certain type of weakness. How can you exploit it? What makes this weakness so effective? Multiply the effectiveness of something weak by studying their strengths. In strength lies weakness. Heavyweight lifters can be bad at cardio, and brains can beat brawn. Strength is weak against speed. If you unplug a stereo, it can no longer function. These examples are some of the billions of ways we can defeat something.

When you discover something that might hurt someone or something, determine whether the weakness will last. Will a tolerance be built to suppress the weakness? Don't attack if you are not 100 percent sure the outcome will be victory. Is there more than one way to damage whatever is causing you trouble?

Instead of using what you know, have a little patience and determine whether someone has the same information. What they will do with it? Has this mode of attack been done already? You are pulling the strings at this point. If you know the weakness of something, you can figure out how the strengths are being used to cover up the weakness. You head off any recourse and solve the dilemma once you begin an assault. You already know what plan B is.

DON'T EXPECT TO BE MOTIVATED

There will be times that seem better if you quit. Those are the times that should get you excited. It's time to do something different. If things are boring, miserable, or worse, take it in stride. Take in the misery and rejoice in the fact that you are on the right course. Your actions are contributing so much good. You have a clear path to work on the things you need to get done.

When walking down a quiet street, take in the peaceful atmosphere. You don't have to deal with noise and bitter elements that cause you to look the other way. You have a strategy to focus on what you want. When no one is around, you have work to do. That is the best time to do overtime. If you have children, a wife, pets, or other responsibilities, someone will wait until it's quiet. When everyone is asleep, no one needs anything. You have all your attention on your goal. When it gets too quiet and lonely, look in the mirror and be happy. Nothing is standing in your way. That emptiness, misery, and boringness is your spirit telling you to get a move on.

DON'T JUDGE A PERSON BY WHERE HE DRINKS BUT BY THE WAY THEY HOLD IT

People come in all shapes and sizes, and you will always have to face someone doing something you might not approve of. It's not what happens; it is the way things happen. Sometimes you have to let people know what the situation is and how you feel—and then sit back and observe what happens.

When someone disagrees with you, they will display it—but it might not be the way you want to receive it. If someone lets you know how they feel respectfully, there is nothing you can do but accept it. Humble yourself when accepting someone's remarks and feelings toward you. Love comes in all shapes and sizes. It can hurt your feelings, but you can take it in stride.

A message is a message, and the wisdom comes from listening, recognizing, and understanding why you got it. Another way to understand someone is to observe how these people hold information.

Alcohol is the truth serum. Get enough of it in your system, and you will see who is who. Fear and anger will do the same thing.

Try to learn how people keep information to themselves. A cracked jar can hold no fluid. Some people are damaged, and trusting them with anything valuable would be a crime.

DON'T PUNISH PEOPLE UNTIL YOU KNOWS ALL THE DETAILS

People will swear up and down that things would've been different. In the end, you should expect the same result. If somebody really was on your side, they wouldn't need to hear anything about you unless it came from your mouth. When it comes to giving away valuable information, do it at your own discretion.

Telling all of your business should not be necessary to preserve a friendship. Once people find what they are looking for, that's it. The betrayal will happen because you spilled your sand to unworthy people. Don't be surprised if they stab you in the back. Information will reveal itself in due time. You don't have to share insignificant things. If it's meant to be discovered, it will be. You just have to trust the time it takes to happen. Save as many details about your life as you can. Those who know more about you should be held to higher expectations.

DO THE MATH

Two plus two will always equal four. Don't try to change how things happen. When you come across bullshit, let it go. Just add fuel to the fire. Plenty of events will take place without you knowing why. It's easy to say the other person is wrong. Begin your detective work. Most events, attacks, assaults, and maneuvers have a pattern. They will come one after the other, and you will count them in the order in which they came.

Your ride across town is late, and you missed the meeting, which caused a financial burden. Your friend is late to the party, and when he gets there, he doesn't have the right drink because the store was closed. He is not dressed properly. You can tell he was screwed before he left the house. Whatever the problem was, it started at the house. That is where you should look for clues. You're going to be hit one day, but do not to lose focus on the tasks that need completion. In life, it's a numbers game. Don't forget it. You talk to enough females? You get the date. You save up enough money? You get the desire. You do enough workouts? You get the body. Numbers add up and work in your favor. Concentrate on the sequence, the timing, and the outcome.

DON'T REPEAT YOUR MISTAKES

Don't make the same mistake twice. If you do, don't let it be a costly one. You better pay attention. Don't let the same thing happen to you over and over. Take heed in the mistakes you make with people, transactions, and interactions. Certain people repeat the same things—even if it is with a different person. The thought process has a different vessel. It's still the same bad intention and bad idea. Start looking at the outcomes of meeting people. The same message can repeat with different individuals. Be good to yourself. Don't teach yourself the same lesson over and over. Learn from your mistakes—and don't repeat them.

See people believe the same shit can come from two different sources. The most beautiful people—and the ugliest ones—can have the same motives in trying to do good or bad by you. Stop getting caught up in looks. Don't start with physical appeal. Think of what a relationship can do for you. It's up to you to let the same type of person, place, situation, or scenario burn you. The hardest thing is letting go of people you can't trust. Some of them will put on performances that should receive awards. Those are the worst. It's okay to not like someone, but trying to be a different person to infiltrate, deceive, or destroy a person is in a whole different league of hatred. Close your eyes and wave goodbye if you have to.

DON'T DEPEND ON YOUR EYES

Life can be deceiving. It can full of deception and misleading information. The most deceptive parts of the body are the mind and the eyes. The first to be attacked will be your mind. The mind is a terrible thing to waste. People will use all kinds of gestures and movements to throw you off. They are trying to trick you into believing one thing and losing sight of another.

Some people say the hand is quicker than the eye, but that is not true. The hands are quicker than the eye. If someone has the goal of hitting you, they already know what they want to do. Before saying hello, they have planned out what they want to do to you. By the time you realize it, the blow is already in motion. Be aware of what's going on around you at all times.

Not knowing what people's intentions are can be costly. The average person thinks one step ahead, but you think eight or ten steps ahead. It's better to be safe than sorry. Try to control the ideas that come to your mind. Don't let your mind run away with the things you obsess over because you can't control your thoughts. Always remain calm before you react. Trying to figure out a solution and upsetting yourself at the same time will only make you more upset. Stay true to yourself, be bright, and believe in yourself. Don't wander off in your mind. Wait and be patient. The answers will come to you. Keep an ear to the ground to listen for the voices of others.

DRESS CODE

A dress code reflects a person's business or personal activities. It conveys a message of professionalism and business savvy, and not everyone has a specific dress code. It is important to understand how influential clothing is and the message it conveys. From a soldier to a plumber, clothing delivers the first message about who you are and what you represent. You should have a few garments to match any situation and scenario that comes about. This will give you options. Have a couple of track outfits, a few nice dress shirts, some slacks, a couple of belts, a pair of tennis shoes, and a pair of dress shoes. Don't forget a watch.

Your attitude should always reflect the clothing you wear. If you wear a suit, it should be hard to get you to make a bad face. The suit will give you such a superior mentality that you can't do anything but focus on the positive. If you feel down about something, try getting dressed up in your favorite outfit and walking around the house. Take care of the problem. This puts you in a positive flow, breaks down any bad energy, and helps you develop positive energy and happiness.

EAT WHAT'S ON YOUR PLATE

Don't get caught up in the mystery of what others are doing. Only worry about the most important person in your life. You can't let the enemy distract you from what you have to do. When you take your eyes off what is important, things can get out of control. Imagine being at a dinner table and staring at someone else's plate. Eventually your food will get cold. Be careful about what you do at the dinner table. Don't reach for another person's plate. The key is to only be concerned about you. What's on someone's plate might not be as good for you as it is for them. Some dinners are buffets, and others are a three-course meals. Learn the difference between feeding off of the same source and getting up from the table when your resources run out.

Greed can be the destruction of you if you are not prepared. Share when it's appropriate. Keep that blade close when it's appropriate.

ENERGY

"I don't want that shit on me. I'm not trying to have that bullshit in my life." Don't say this about people. Energy is real. Energy is all around, and if you are not careful, your energy can be corrupted. What good is a battery with no energy? If you have a battery that goes out, it can damage your device. A negative person can make an opportunity fade like a light. Keep yourself around people who make you feel good. The people around you should intimidate you. You should feel like you are in over your head. Keeping up with them is a way to increase your status and amp your energy. The metal inside the earth is turning and causing electromagnetic waves that affect gravity. What type of energy is produced by humans with the turning of our blood? We produce energy—whether are aware of it or not—and our thoughts dictate what it does in our lives. Be careful of the company you keep. If they give you a bad feeling, look into it. If necessary, get them away from you. With bad energy, you will vibe with the negatives of the universe. That might not be beneficial to you in the long run. Don't attract situations you don't like or that don't match what you stand for.

ENJOY THE RIDE

Smile! Smile once more. Keep smiling through it all. During the ups and downs, the good and bad and ugly, keep enjoying you. Be happy for the specific stress and frustration during this adventure. Own every minute of it—and appreciate the growth it puts you through. You're going to enjoy some things and not others. You might have to plan a new segment and become someone better. Like all things in this world, that is not going to be free. The price you pay is the price it takes to go out and become something better than you were. A positive attitude is the best way to start. Be thankful for the problems you have and not the ones you don't have. Picture yourself where you want to be. Imagine accomplishing everything you want to do in life. Do you see how that feels? Imagine being successful and achieving your hopes and dreams—even the really small ones. After climbing the mountain of success, things should be in a better perspective. Why are you paying attention to things that don't matter? Freedom should be on your mind at all times. Let everything go and smile. Take a step in the right direction. Step over obstacles and people who won't help you become something in this world.

EQUITY

Equity is the value of your investment in something. Most people assume stocks and shares, but what about people? What equity could you hold within a person? Motivations, affirmations, daily calls, counseling, support. If like what someone is doing, you need to get with the program and support them. When you find someone you believe in, give them your wholehearted support and don't look back. To have some equity in something is to have a stake in the production and growth of something. Some of the responsibility for moving forward rests with you. What you do with it is up to you. You can linger around someone who is struggling without offering a helping hand. The chance to encourage people to finish the course should never be misused or ignored. If you spent years sleeping on the floor of someone's place, slept in cars, or endured hardships, was a person steadily preaching the message of success? That should not go unnoticed. The person who ignores that type of support will get what's coming to them. Placing your faith in the wrong person or venture will result in a negative outcome. The choice is yours. Take the time to learn the ropes and look for good prospects.

ETHOS, PATHOS, AND LOGOS

Ethos appeals to the ethical appeal of someone by convincing an audience of the author's credibility or character. Pathos, an appeal to the emotions of the audience, elicits feelings that already reside in them. Logos is an appeal to reason or logic by using facts or evidence. These are the three forms of persuasion. Derived from Greek philosophers, the types of persuasion are used to convey messages and deliver information. It's best if you learn how to use the different types of persuasion because other people most definitely try to use them on you. These might be forms you already use. It is like going to driver's school and learning what the blinker does or what the knobs are called. It's takes a little bit of research and knowledge to understand different forms of communication. You can learn the skills to reject the persuasions. Even though you might not be a good speaker, the art of knowing how to persuade is important for getting ahead, especially in a leadership position. Do not think others won't try to pass themselves off on you with the same skills. Study a little bit and perfect the skill that works best for you. You can learn how to mix and match. Ethos and pathos are used by toddlers to convince their parents to do things. Practice these techniques and bring yourself one step closer to achieving what you want out of life.

EVEN THE ODDS

It's all about the participation you put into things that relate and don't relate to you. If something is going on that you don't agree with, let it go. To get on the same level of someone, acknowledge that they are a worthy foe. A foe worth responding to is a foe capable of defeating you. The more you ignore people who cannot harm you, the more they can't.

To cause everlasting damage, you must hit the person the same way they hit you. Imagine that your enemy is throwing things at you. You want to kick that person's ass. You have to climb a ladder to thrash that person in front of everyone once and for all. Depending on your circumstances, only you know how tall that ladder is before you can go up there to begin a proper bout.

The best thing to do when faced with the issue of when to strike is make sure it is on the same playing field. Before you get on that playing field, how far is it from you? How do you get there? What is missing? Can you do damage at the same level? Somebody with more assets and resources than you has an advantage. They might be doing damage, but the damage can be less harmful if you don't respond until you get high enough to put them in their place. It might take time to get to the same level, but when you get up there, you can hit them with whatever you have saved up. It might be old, but it won't even matter. The wisdom and intelligence it takes to be on the same level comes after reaching that point. By then, you can do three or four times the damage with the same data. How many uses does a sharp pencil have? Do you see my point? On the same level, the odds of hitting them where it hurts are much greater.

EVERYBODY DESERVES ONE MORE SHOT

You decide whether to trust someone, but you need people in life. Even if you observe someone's deception and learn from them, you need to know what people are after and what you need to protect. Sometimes you have to give people one chance. People will show you their hands, and you want to know what cards they are going to deal next time.

Unless the ultimate betrayal has occurred, you need to keep an eye on people who have information or valuable assets. Even in a casual situation, learn to maneuver around people. People aren't invincible. Everyone is vulnerable to some degree. The key is to know how to defend yourself against these individuals if necessary. Even if you just prolong the inevitable, you have to find out what you need to know before the situation ends. Keep a close eye on anyone who would betray you. If they genuinely don't like you, then your acceptance will come swiftly or fade in a hurry. If they have a hidden agenda, take caution. Only provide the opportunity to return with a cost and the threat of immediate termination.

EVERYTHING BUILDS UP

When it all boils down to it, the end game is what's important. However, the road to get there will be as dramatic as you allow it to be. When you're climbing the ladder of success or pushing up a mountain of goals, the buildup is more important than the actual climax. The more effort you put into the something, the more it should return to your expectations. You should benefit on the journey, but the journey itself should be a prize.

Exercising, cleaning an engine, studying for a test, and creating a better memory require putting one foot in front of the other. You must break down your goal into small tasks. Instead of one big great thing being done in one day, turn it into a daily routine.

Start with what you think is the most important thing. If building a car is important to you, map out everything you need to do. Start building toward your goal. A house starts with the construction of the basement or the first floor. Once the foundation is made, you put up the walls. The key to a good building is a proper foundation. An athlete works hard on the body, the mind, and the diet. Start with the first things first. A great outside comes from a great inside. Imagine yourself in a street race. Would you prefer a car that performs great on the outside or the inside? Which is the most important?

EXTRA HELP

Extra help will always come in handy. People will like you more when you accept their help. Extra help usually comes at a cheaper price and has benefits. Extra means something you receive beyond your needs. Find a way for people to help you. Do not make yourself more accessible, but if your business is geared toward gaining more attention, allow someone to help you. Be careful about who you bring aboard to assist you. When you let people help you in the beginning, it frees If somebody wants to help, you should really consider it. People who choose to help out of kindness are genuine. No matter what they contribute, make sure you appreciate each and every gift. Do yourself a favor and learn why they gave you a specific gift in the first place.

Though it is not something you'd practice regularly, manipulating the help you need is a good way to receive the assistance you require. If you need a spare tire and someone offers a ride, that is extra help. It is outside of your requirements, yet it still helps you reach your ultimate goal. When people assist you, what you need help with should be perfectly clear. Extra help should make things go much faster. You know it's helping if they are precise in their assumptions of what you need.

EXCITED FOR WHAT?

The person who is trying to piss you off is guaranteed to be disappointed by someone else someday. Don't let their initial behavior make you angry. They will get what's coming to them eventually— all you have to do is wait. You analyze their behavior and observe the environment. If the environment does not accept them 100 percent, something will happen one day. People might want to get a rise out of you. They are pulling your strings. They ignore people to gain your attention. The person is trying to get you excited. Continue to watch them. Insults should not elevate your emotions. Words are just words. If someone says something to get you excited, don't pay attention to them. That person is losing their mind. It's a sign of weakness when people get you to behave differently.

FALSE ADVERTISEMENT

People on both sides of the fence will have something bad to say about you. It's inevitable. They will say bad things about you. They will try to downplay everything you are doing. They will put down your accomplishments. Don't let it get you. Forget everybody who says something bad about you. As long as they keep talking, don't worry about it.

A bad commercial gets more attention than a good one. You will certainly remember a bad one. Do not befriend someone who makes a false advertisement. They are telling people bad things about you. They don't mean well. The negative energy starts with the mind, the voice, the words, and the action. Negative people are breeding for you disaster. Let them shine light on you from a distance. If they use words, they will use actions. Those people are itching to reveal a bad side of you. Don't let them get close to you or anyone else. They will poison people around you. At any given moment, they will strike.

They will strike at you when everyone is appealing to you. You will gain the approval of people, they might want it.

FEAR

Fear is an unpleasant emotion caused by the belief that someone or something is dangerous. It is likely to cause pain. Fear is not real. It is a made-up decision. You are challenged to work and feel pressure to accomplish your goals. Fear is a cross between surprise and stress.

Sometimes fear helps you survive. It activates a fight-or-flight response. That is the basic answer.

An intellectual person should investigate why he or she is feeling that way. They might cause you to stress, but you can handle whatever comes your way. You can control how you react to fear. You can't always go in guns blazing, but you can strategize and come up with a weakness.

If people paid good money to hear you talk, they are one step closer to becoming your friend. The last thing anyone is going to do is boo you or disrespect you. All you have to do is go out there. It is that easy. Look at the logic you used to break things down.

If you said everything you have to say to a person who knows you care about them, the only thing left is to get past the actual surgery. If push comes to shove, you will know that the person knew the truth and went in with a peaceful mind-set. A lot won't go your way in life. How you handle it and take on the problems will determine the outcome for you. When you feel fear setting in, know that something is threatening you.

FEAR AND GREED

There will always be a turnaround, there will always be a climax, and the tide will always rise and sink. Be prepared when it does. It does not have to be greed that you use in times of stress; it can be anger, fear, happiness, or patience. Whatever you physically feel the need for is what you use. During any struggle, examine why that is. No matter what it is. A sinking ship has a hole. Plug the hole—or abandon ship. The choice is yours.

The fearful have already determined what they will do. What will you do? The turning point might not come in your lifetime. Will you remain diligent and do what it takes to have a breakthrough? Will you fall by the wayside? Only the strong will survive, and only the brave will be rewarded.

Fortune favors the bold. You have to get off your ass and face your fears. Be on guard—even when everything is going as planned. The new set of problems has not arrived yet. Be on guard—even when everything is going as it should be going. Even if things don't turn for the worse, you still want to be prepared.

Throughout history, problems have led to major events and created heroes. You can't have one without the other. Preparation is the victor in any circumstance. If you are a hero, stay on guard and turn any problem into an opportunity to create a solution. The time will come for everyone to prove themselves at the right moment.

FIRE UNDER YOUR FEET

The real strength you're going to need is the ability to take the bad you experience and use it as fuel. When something bad occurs, your goal is to ask yourself why it is happening in the first place. Why is something like this or that happening to you in the first place? Why is it happening? When something bad happens, enjoy the pain and say thank you for it. Be grateful for the pain you receive. When something bad happens, be glad.

When buying a car, your credit needs to be fixed. That is a sign that you're on the right track and need to adjust your approach. After finally purchasing that vehicle, you might get pulled over because the car brings about a lot of unwanted attention. That is a problem that comes with the territory. You get what you ask for. The problems that come with your goals are the ones that help you build a better version of yourself. Be thankful for the good people and the bad people you come across. The bad people are just passing by to teach you a lesson. Learn from every mistake and take note of every encounter.

FILTERING

You should have a system to filter through people and activities. Like water through a pot with holes in it, you need to catch what you want and separate the rest. Authentic people and creative works are rare. If networking is your goal, set up a get-together party. Use that party to arrange a social event with the people you are more interested in. It's a double event, and the goal is to separate people. Use the internet to search through your options.

It's okay to be particular about things that have your interest. You can use all kinds of situations and scenarios to create a perfect circle. The best way to find someone like you is to look for people who have been through the same things you've been through. If they have the same attitude, take things to the next stage.

FLOW

The art of staying in the groove is when you're doing something and lose track of time. This can occur at any given moment. Some moments are spent with others, and other times are spent alone. You should always try to get into the flow of things. Losing track of time is not a bad thing. It means losing yourself in the moment, and people want to hold on to time for no reason.

As you get older, people will say, "Where did the years go? How did I lose track of time?" They get caught in the flow of what they are doing. Think of a moment a song became your favorite song. What were you doing? Where were you? Who were you with? Those are the moments you hold onto. Even if what you are doing is distracting, be sure to do something that you really enjoy. Do not be afraid to let the time go by quickly. A lot of times, people try to hold on to the present by paying attention to every minute that goes by. Don't do that. Focus on the joy you develop along the way. Everybody gets older—some quicker than others—but that doesn't mean you can enjoy yourself. Document and record as many happy times as you can. That way, you can reminisce in the future.

FOOL ME ONCE

Are you shitting me? Fool me once, shame on you. Fool me twice, shame on me. The opposition will do the same thing over and over. You must think I'm really stupid. This is the attitude one must have to survive the repetitive nature of those who are trying to get in the way of progress. You will come across the same attacks, but like a kid who no longer needs his training wheels, the system gets routine. Once you're able to recognize the same treachery, it will start to develop a pattern.

After observing those you feel are not in your corner, people will perform the deeds of destruction. It's one thing for a close friend or acquaintance to suddenly betray your trust, but if it is your parents or relatives, it might shock you. They might have good intentions and not trust the route you've chosen. Don't be surprised by anything you experience during your rise to the top. Living above your station will rub many people the wrong way, especially those who knew you from the beginning. You had a dream and were bragging to everybody about how you were going to get that dream car and house one day. Pay close attention. That behavior could come from jealousy or envy. Deal with it no matter who it manifests from. The best way to avoid a conflict is to be quiet and swift. You shouldn't let anyone know what's going on in your mind. Assess the problem and come up with a solution so both sides can separate. You can escape harm's way without being detected.

FOOLS WILL BE FOOLS

In this long journey, you will come across a fool who believes he or she has all the answers. You can't reason with those people, and you can't communicate with them. There is no way to get through to these people. The definition of a fool is someone who is unwise. There is no sense in getting caught up with these people. They are out for trouble. Nine times out of ten, they're going to get what's coming to them.

The more you try, the more you are going to suffer. If anyone gets too close to you and behaves like an idiot, drop them. The most dangerous thing about a foolish person is ambition. They get into all kinds of shit, and they will jump into more the next day. Not knowing when to stop is their greatest weakness. Listen to your gut with someone who behaves like a fool. It's always going to end badly with these people. Those people can also be selfish. They take so many risks and put you and everyone around them in jeopardy. Be cautious when they come around. Leave them be and move on as soon as you can. When trying to decipher a fool, you only make a fool of yourself.

FORCE

Strength or energy is an attribute of physical action or movement. Force can be used to go with the flow or against the flow. It requires much more energy to go against the grain. When you disagree with someone, it can get personal.

Using force requires exerting yourself beyond the normal means of negotiation. Force is a form of a threat, and it never cooperates with its user. It will render you unable to take the same route in communicating with people. Once you apply force in any negotiation, the terms of communication change for good, especially in a business setting. Threats and other forms of coercion will automatically shift you from being in control to being on the losing end. You should never have to apply force to anything verbal. If you have to use force on people, you shouldn't be involved with them. If that is a necessity, put a time limit on the presence of such requirements.

When asking someone to do something for you, there should be no threat or force unless you absolute have to. If so, limit the time and use of force. When using force, be as accurate as possible. Be precise and get to the point immediately. If somebody requires an ass beating, apply that punishment swiftly, promptly, and with due cause. When the conflict is over, that person or entity should be down for the count. Like a cool, calm, and collected martial artist, you should know exactly what to do and when to do it. The use of force can be verbal. Don't exercise grace before applying force.

FORMATION

When you're in formation, you are developing character. The trick is practice, and the character it takes to maintain your skill starts to grow. If you want to be a boxer, you should start practicing your fighting skills. In addition to training your body, you must create the ideal body. You will discover what time to go to bed—even though you like watching martial arts movies before bed.

When you wake up, you have the techniques to focus on. Begin the day with your new routines. One of your goals should be to perform the new skills and habits you need to develop and maintain the level of achievement you are looking to keep.

Stop associating with people who might cause your emotions to rise. Even if they were your friends, they might have bad habits and create a negative atmosphere that involves starting fights. Drink a sports beverage before a match, water during the match, and milk after the match. Maintain peak performance. If you spend all your money in one day, it will be a problem the next day. Experience and conditioning help you realize you need to maintain a certain income to survive.

FRAME BY FRAME

Sometimes the situation may come down to whether you remember certain details. It is crucial to pay close attention to the details. You don't always have to be in trouble to notice things that appear out of order. Whenever something occurs, you want to be able to remember the details. People can be forgetful during times of questioning.

It is be easy to remember details like winning the lottery or watching an important game. A comrade can draw a blank in an instant if things get really bad. Two guys might say they don't know or don't recall something. Depending on the stress and pressure level, they could be lost in the sauce.

Somebody might ask, "What was your friend wearing when he discovered his winning ticket?" That can be disastrous. If the winnings are based on that question, your friends might forget. If it is a crime, your friends' focus might be on self-preservation. They might remember all about you to shift the focus off of themselves.

The military teaches you to control your emotions and remain focused. Unfortunately, it takes more than just watching and observing to remember details. You must be calm, cool, and collected. Your emotions should be stable and not interfere with anything that runs through your mind.

Practice trying to remember small things that occur during the day. You begin by writing the details of what happened during the day. This will teach your brain to focus. This might seem like a useless practice, but if you can recall the same situation, it could help you. All you have to do is remember what happened and fix it. Once you learn something, you can recall it physically and mentally.

FREE ADVERTISING

All publicity is good publicity—even in the worst times. When people acknowledge your existence, it is a good thing. It is a cause for attention. If people are talking about you, that means they are interested in you. Let them be that way. As long as it doesn't bring danger to you, who cares what people think? It's not up to them to decide how you live your life.

Your haters are paying attention to you around the clock. A hater is going to make sure everything about you is known and documented. A hater keeps all the facts about you up to date. Don't waste time arguing with people who like talking about you. It's a no-brainer.

A hater is more obsessed with you than a fan is. A fan is going to comment on a post you make on social media. A hater is going analyze every portion of it and share it with other people to get a reaction. A fan might do the same, but they will not be so critical of your every move. Cherish the people who talk about you. It means they're interested in you.

FRONT TO BACK

You always want to benefit from a deal on both ends. When you buy a product for your store, you make a profit on the sale. To make money on the front end, you should be receiving an incentive to make the purchase. Whatever you make after the sale is the back end. If someone tries to rip you off, it's going to be at the front end. If their integrity is low, it will be at the back end. The integrity is low if you have to question if the goods and services are up to par. High integrity means they have a good product. You're likely guaranteed to make a profit, but they will try to rip you off in the count or the pricing.

Try to gain a discount on the front end. If you save money on the purchase and make the same profit, you change the bottom line. The savings will accumulate eventually. This grants you the ability to make a double purchase in the future. If you save additional funds, they build up over time.

A bad tenant might give you money to move in, get evicted, and damage the place. You will have to pay to fix it. They got you on the back end because that money you took from them is going back into fixing the damages. You're at a loss on the back end because you have to deduct money from the arrangement. Any deal, agreement, arrangement, or exchange has a front and a back end. The front end is the negotiations, and the back end is the collections, profits, and sales.

FUEL

Everything we do is fuel that will contribute to us. The bag of chips might be a builder of bad cholesterol, and the sports jacket you find so appealing could lead to you being a dollar short in the future.

You don't have to be in a ship, but your life is like riding in a ship. Every action you make is contributing to the speed and direction of the vehicle. A bad choice leads to less fuel and the ship slowing down. The right choices lead to the ship moving quickly toward where you want to be in life.

You should already be able to tell who is not supposed to be on your ship and who is. If you have to question anybody's motives, they should be removed immediately. They are only going to cause harm in the future, especially if the ship is moving toward clear seas. It will be taking on water. As you are moving along, the ship takes on water. This is fine if you face rough waters, but the ship will need maintenance.

If the ship starts taking on water, you can't predict what how people will do. Some people will cause as many problems as they can for others. That is none of your concern. You can't change these people if they don't want to be helped. All you can do is focus on you and what you are doing for yourself.

Some person try to sink the ship they are riding in—even if it brings the risk of drowning themselves. They will try to stop you from succeeding. People who will sabotage you don't care about themselves. A ship brings perspective about what is important. To keep your ideas floating and moving along, you must monitor all the dynamics. Not everyone will make it, and if your crew shouldn't be considered allies, you should send them on their way. A life raft can be something that keeps them floating while they move away from you.

GAUGES

The appearance and disappearance of a person, place, or thing can be an indication of an opportunity, a meeting, money, food, or something you want to buy. All these scenarios are times to save energy and rethink what you are interested in.

Whenever something goes wrong, step back and look at it as an opportunity to do something different. Take it as a gauge that is depleted because of the time you took to execute the opportunity. Go after something or stop and wait. Never get mad when you miss out on something. Just ask, "What else can I do with the time I have?" If some food gets eaten at a dinner, the first thing you do is look for something else you want on the table. Do the same thing with any opportunity for success or gift. Go after the second choice. Don't do anything without a second choice and a third choice. If the chance runs out, go to the next thing. Have an interest in your second choice. If you miss out, it won't be as disappointing. It can be a bit exciting to see what happens if the chance goes away.

GET IT 80 PERCENT RIGHT AND MAKE CORRECTIONS LATER

About 20 percent of your activities will account for 80 percent of your results. The most crucial decisions you make will come from the first actions you make toward a goal and mission. The most crucial point of your work will come in the first twenty minutes because the first tasks are the most important.

If your life depended on it, what would be the most important thing for you to do? That will determine where you should start. Focus on getting what's most important done first. The value in what you do is important. Sometimes the small gestures are the most favored in victory. Passion is the driving force for the most successful and the defense against the most sinister. You have to break down the most important values, contributions, intentions. Your first child will be the career you choose. You can refer to this as a baby because you know what you need to keep a baby alive. That is what you choose, and that is what you will use to propel yourself forward when all else fails and all your visions disappear.

GIFTS WRAPPED IN PROBLEMS

You should be glad about the problems you have. They problems are specific to you and who you are. If anybody else were to have your problems, would they want them? If you were to trade problems with someone else, would you want to keep them? That is something you should really ask yourself. Sooner or later, you will face problems you wish somebody else had.

Recognize that you are the one who made them. Someone took advantage of you and made problems for you, but you can fix them. You will never be perfect, but you can come close by allowing yourself to fall short sometimes. You can draw someone out with bait. Bait can be an opportunity or a weakness. It's up to you to discover how far you are willing to go to reach your ultimate potential.

Police departments and the military use Tasers as a last test before graduation. It serves as a reminder of what you put other people through. You will know what you are up against if that weaponry gets in the wrong hands. The same response should be given to people who try to gain the upper hand against you by using things you're not prepared for. The way to overcome a lot of what you might face is to ignore it. What are they doing, and what are they not doing? What are they not setting up for?

When problems occur, they are weaknesses you must fix. Unless you want shit to continue, resolve the problem in a way it can never return. Take your time. The problem took time to arrive, and it will take twice as long come up with a permanent solution. Thank the problem for coming to you in the first place. It is a person, place, or thing that is no longer fit to be around you.

GOALS ARE LONG-TERM DESTINATIONS, AND OBJECTIVES AND MISSIONS ARE SHORT-TERM DESTINATIONS

Always break down what you want into small steps. Write down your goals. There should be steps that lead to completing the task. If you want a car, you need money, a plate, tags, insurance, and a license. If the list is in reverse order, then reverse engineer what you need to do. The main thing is to write down the it will take to accomplish that goal. Objectives are side missions. These will help you achieve your goal.

The objectives should be broken down in steps. That way, you can thoroughly execute what needs to be done. Don't just write down your goals. Envision them in your head. Each time you walk out that front door, picture the task being completed. When you think about things that need to be done, picture the reactions and responses of the people involved.

Nothing should catch you off guard—not even traffic—because you write down the time and money you need to spend on something. You can never be too sure about anything. When you take the time to calculate and figure things out, you get a good sense of what needs to be done. Most people do not prepare that way. They go about doing things without trying to gather as much information as possible. That will matter when you finish something important to you. Gather all the data and properly execute everything that needs to be done.

GOSSIP

The most important thing you can when people are negative is be quiet. Don't participate in negative talk. The words of anyone else should never leave your lips for any reason. No one is perfect. Don't try to persecute your fellow man with negative thoughts and words.

If you don't like someone, only that person should know about it. Nobody else should have a clue about the issue is between you and the other person. The best way to get over on people is to keep your mouth shut. People will try to flush you and see if you have a problem with another person. If someone offers you a chance to talk about someone else, pay attention to that person and say nothing about anybody, especially since words travel.

Your opinion about anyone else is yours and yours alone. Don't waste time talking about other people. It will not work out to your benefit. When someone is gossiping about other people, you know they will soon talk about you as well. Don't give them anything to say. A gossiping person shouldn't be trusted with information. That doesn't mean you shouldn't listen from time to time and learn about a person. People are followers, and they learn things the wrong way, but a few interactions with a person can come back in the words of other people.

Be cautious of how others look at a person and the people they hang around. They will eventually look at you the same way.

GREED

Avoid greed. Why ask for more than what you need? You don't need to do that. All you have to do is go after what is required. The minimum is enough. Always seek what you need rather than what you want. Set a number or goal just above what you need to get done—and go after it. That way, if you get a little more, you won't know what to do with it.

The most important thing is to stay away from people who are greedy. You're going to come across people who want it all and who are completely gluttonous. Stay away from these people because that money is going to lead them into a trap, a bad business deal, or an unsafe position. Money is nothing more than a means to build a solid foundation.

Don't chase money—and pay attention to opportunities that are presented to you. You always want a way to make your own money. It's better to have the ability to make your own money. If you are your own boss, when you start making money, treat yourself to something nice. Don't spend more than 15 percent of your money. Save the rest or buy something cheaper. Be smart about what you buy. Be frugal in your spending and hold on to more than what you spend. Do not chase after something for just profit. If you believe in what you do, money and opportunities will present themselves. When starting out, stretch your resources. If you get three, only use half of it. When you get five, it will be more like a surplus.

GRIN AND BEAR IT

In life, sometimes you need to grin and bear it. There are people who really want to see you suffer. Do not allow them to infect your spirit with hate and envy. No matter what happens, allow them to do what they are doing and move forward. Don't allow people to distract you with bullshit. A distraction will keep you from staying the course.

Some people feel like they have nothing to live for, and they will try to sabotage whatever is going on. Don't let them. Think of it as hardening your skin. After someone does the same thing repeatedly, keep it out of mind. If a toddler hits you, you will probably laugh. A child can really do no harm.

Have the endurance to make it to where you are going. Let go of everything that is not hindering your progress. In a sauna, your ability to deal with heat increases until you can take more than another person. The same will happen in life. As long as the actions people take are no threat to you, forget about them. They won't matter in the future anyway.

GROW ON THE GO

At the gym, you immediately notice who has been attending for some time and who is visiting. The efforts that everyone puts in—from cardio to weightlifting to meditation to yoga—accumulate into the body's health and appearance. Your body will become fit, and your mind will become durable.

Things people say and do will not bother you as much because your body will transmit that energy from the mind to other parts of your body. In before-and-after pictures, appearances change—and so does the way people look and feel toward others. People screaming at you for long periods of time will make you want to calm down. The noise causes issues with the senses and conditions the mind.

Once you perfect your craft, nothing should faze you anymore. Athletes, musicians, artists, teachers, students, and factory workers have a certain level of mental growth. The mind becomes aware of its surroundings. A threshold of reality is gained. Some call it common sense, but common sense is not common. People think about making a purchase, how long a meal will last, how much it will cost, and if it is worth it.

On some level, everybody will think about money. Everyone shares that experience. Keep on growing and remain calm.

GO WITH ALL YOUR HEART

It doesn't matter who you are around. In unknown territory, become anyone's friend if need be. You should be able to fit in and take over in a small amount of time. Most areas are the same, and the most essential element is communication. Without some sort of communication, nowhere would be accessible. If you are going somewhere dangerous, throw this information out the window. You shouldn't be anywhere unpredictable.

Be careful when expressing yourself to other people, and always allow someone to convey your message for you in other places. When trying to convince people of a different terrain who you are and how you are as a person, let someone else get the crowd's attention. Birds of a feather walk together. Do overuse yourself when gaining approval. Use people from the area. Don't go somewhere you're not familiar with and try to relate to people who can't vibe with your output. Be sure to leave your message behind. People will cherish it after you leave. Leave a message that will inspire people to follow in your footsteps.

HABITS

Habits are settled or regular tendencies or practices, especially ones that are hard to give up. If you like the pleasure of people, you need to figure out why you like those types of pleasures. Intoxications, excitements, and brutal intentions are some of things that make up habits. You have to control yourself, which is easier said than done.

The most important change is figuring what triggers your interest. If looking at things that cause you to lust starts up your motors, perhaps you should avoid them. You need to find the root of the issue. Everything has a beginning. A puddle of water comes from a hole. A hole is created through the ruptures of a defense. A rupture is created through the pressure of a point you haven't analyzed for weaknesses.

You have to know how to fix a quality or trait you do not want to continue. It starts with what you no longer like. The way you are living is predicated on your values and the way you treat yourself. You have to be smart about the way you treat yourself and others. You have to be smart about the way you see yourself and others, and you have to evaluate yourself through the lens of what it is necessary to survive. You have to take joy in what you give yourself. When you shed something negative, give yourself a smile.

HARBOR YOUR OWN STRENGTHS

Everything you go through can be used to help you grow. No matter the circumstances, every challenge you face gives you strength. The people you meet are there for you to learn from. Being lied to, deceived, betrayed, disappointed, angered, cornered, or ambushed are all learning lessons, but they are character-building elements. These situations and scenarios should be looked at as gaining abilities.

What doesn't kill you makes you stronger. When a bone breaks, it heals and forms harder and stronger. Your mind increases after every experience, and things that repeat get old. Use it to your advantage. The average person cannot sit for long in a room with no distractions? If you drop your phone, it might break. You might have to wait to get a new one, During that time, you're taking a small break. You didn't ask for it, but is forced on you nonetheless. Breaking the next phone will be an easier transition.

Look at everything you go through as a lesson and be thankful for the fortitude to have been there and done that. Sit back, study yourself, and evaluate what can help you in the future.

HELPING YOUR ENEMY

This is more difficult than it sounds, and it is different from using bait to find your weaknesses. This is helping the enemy and taking on the consequences of doing so. Allow a person or people to develop exit strategies, which fattens them up. Make them become bigger targets and hit them where it hurts. This is more difficult than it sounds because the outcome can be out of control.

Those people can develop allies, which means more enemies for you. To control this chaos, never lead someone you like around any potential allies. It is deception, and the concept of the unknown can sway someone into not liking you. It's hard, and you should not try it without a guaranteed way of stopping the process in its tracks when the time comes.

Whether on the battlefield, the office, or a sports arena, don't allow someone you don't like into your world. Watch their movements. Keep them guessing. Do let them know what your next move will be. Even though they might think they have the upper hand, they don't.

If you know what they intend to do, set a play for them. The trap must be carefully orchestrated because something unexpected could happen. Never help anyone do anything against you unless you are absolutely sure you have control of their movements and decisions. You should be able to manipulate the people who come and go.

Those people might become allies, and the purpose of this exercise is to stop them in their tracks. The more room you give them to move, the more you control their lives. Don't let the actions in this process embarrass you. As long as you're pulling the strings, closing the curtain is all that matters. Helping your enemy is more than setting them up for elimination. It's about letting them clear the path for you and rooting out the wrong elements. They will attract people you don't want in your life, and they will endure hardships you don't want. Don't interfere with anything they are doing if it's not a means to an end.

HONESTY

Honesty involves telling the truth, but it might benefit you to preserve what you know. It could work out better if you use selective honesty. Nobody said you had to tell the whole truth. What people don't know won't hurt them in the long run. Putting someone else's business out for the world to know or releasing information is extremely harmful.

Trust no one to tell you the complete truth in anything. Remain cautious in your assumptions and opinions. No one should know exactly what you are thinking. They should respect you for telling the truth and knowing right from wrong. Tell someone the information they need to know, but hold off when you can. You don't want to get personal with people when answering their questions. Tell them what they need to know when they need to know it—and nothing more. Avoid conflict at all times, and if you have to, avoid saying anything. People only know as much as you tell them.

HONOR

Being honorable is knowing what is right and what is wrong. Even thieves have a code of ethics. If you don't plan on being an honorable person, come get your refund immediately. I'm sorry for wasting your time. Don't walk out the door again without considering the needs of others. Without doing that, you are incredibly dumb. You are going to need someone one day, and they will need you. The compromise is about how you convince them to help you first.

Love yourself enough to allow people into your heart. Don't shut off the world because of a few bad apples. Be willing to accept a few things. Honor will cost you plenty of time, space, and money, but it will save you from other mistakes. To be honorable is to be above reproach. When people know not to fuck with you, they will think twice about how they speak on your behalf.

When you look out for others, others will come and go. The ones who stay and protect the fountain you provide will be the ones to cup their hands and carry your message. Honor costs nothing to start and gives you all the respect you could ever want. Be responsible with the name you build because a name that holds weight is a name that will stay. Achilles was great warrior, and he had few weaknesses. He respected his foes enough to know what was necessary to suppress them and lower his chances of defeat.

I DON'T LET PEOPLE I'M SMARTER THAN PISS ME OFF

Imagine being at a dinner party or a picnic, and in the middle of a good conversation, you laugh. A baby walks by and spills red punch all over your shoes and pants. Are you going to grab the child and lose your temper? Are you going pick up a cup of punch and throw it on the child? No, you're going to get mad a little bit and move on. The main thing you are going to do is blame yourself. You are going to contemplate how the whole ordeal took place. What could you have done to avoid the mistake? Why did it have to happen to you? When you get home, you will remove the filthy garments.

You need to apply the same thing to every person who tries to piss you off. Did the child ruin your evening—or was it a simple setback? People are going to do a lot of things to upset you—on purpose and accidently—throughout your life. You need to let go of what you have been through and move forward into what could happen if you are not prepared.

Always keep the bigger picture in mind. Keep a spare pair of shoes or pants in your luggage. It can fix things quickly and change everything from a loss to a triumph. The embarrassment is getting to you. It comes from something miniscule. There could be someone at the event who makes you feel powerless, helpless, or vulnerable. Step outside your body for a second to show everyone how tough you are and what you are made of. Calm down, say, "No big deal," and go to the bathroom or borrow some clothes. The key is to regroup your thoughts. That's it!

Do the same thing with each monumental or tiny ordeal you face. It's all in how you perceive the problem. Anybody who fucks with you wants trouble and hasn't thought it all the way through. As an adult, you will calm yourself, see things clearly, analyze what happened, and figure out a solution.

IF IT'S ON, IT'S ON

When it's time to go to war, there are no compromises. Once someone decides to begin a battle with you, it's time to fire both barrels and destroy them. You cannot afford to underestimate anyone, especially on the road to success. They have to be taught not to mess with you or disrespect you in any way, shape, or form. You want a reputation for not tolerating any bullshit from anybody.

Whatever you stand for is a reflection of your business and those you associate with. The second you realize something is a threat, you eliminate that threat. If not for you, do it for those you protect and those who depend on you. When it's all over and done with, what do you want them to say about you? Think about your favorite beverage. Do you think it cares about the opposing soft drinks? Do you think that company was refused by certain vendors because of opposing companies? If you don't put their product on the shelf, there will be problems between that company and the vendor.

In a case of advertising between two companies, each company will handle the other one. You have to be direct when responding to a problem. Sometimes it's the middleman or the opposing management. In personal vendettas, be direct with who you respond to. The person you're attacking might not be the individual who started things. When it's time to handle things, there is no looking back.

IF IT'S WRONG, DON'T DO IT—IF IT'S NOT TRUE, DON'T SAY IT

You are going to face people who are vile, mean, and nasty people. Those people will bring out the worst in you and make you angry. You might want to do bad things to them. They are safe because you do not care. Why are you wasting your time? Stay on the mission and let everyone else say and do what they want.

People tend to want to test the waters to see what you will and won't do. If it's not true, don't say it. Who cares about information that doesn't matter in the first place? Be peaceful, be positive, and always keep love in your heart. If someone pisses you off by accident or on purpose, keep the love in your heart for what you want to create.

It doesn't matter how painful some has made your life, people always get what is coming to them. Just be patient, let them have their way, and do not stop what you are trying to accomplish. Ignore people, let them do what they want, and go about your business.

IF THE ENEMY WANTS TO WIN, LET THEM WIN

The most dangerous dream killer is doubt, and the most dangerous advisor is ego. Never listen to either one of these emotions. They are put in your mind to mix you up. People need to be first in line—and always right, never wrong, and innocent 99 percent of the time.

If you were about to cross a major intersection in heavy traffic, you would stop to look both ways and make sure oncoming traffic was clear. While you are patiently waiting for the cars to clear, some jackass walks up beside you and says, "I'm not waiting for traffic to clear. I'm going now."

At first, you think he joking and say, "Are you kidding? I don't think that is a good idea."

He starts walking forward, and you grab his arm. He shrugs and says, "I'm going—and you can't stop me."

That should be it.

When you let him go, he gets hit and causes a major accident. Who is at fault here? Most people will say it is their fault, beat themselves up about it, and say, "I could've done something more." In reality, what could you have done besides get hurt or killed? That is the problem with most people. Instead of worrying about themselves, they try to be a hero. That will not do. You didn't save the most important person you can value: yourself. Sometimes you have to sit back and let people learn what they can and can't do. That is just the way life is sometimes. Stop thinking you can save everyone—and let them find out the cold, hard truth on their own.

Enemies may think they will triumph over you, but if you play smart, they will not. Instead of boasting that you have the upper hand, let them think whatever they want. The goal is to make it past an obstacle without being struck by oncoming problems. If somebody wants to try to beat the odds, use it to your advantage. You can love and care about people from a distance.

IF YOU BELIEVE IN YOURSELF, YOU CAN HELP YOURSELF

Speak from a positive perspective. If you were trapped in a cage, the first thing you would think of is how to obtain freedom. The cage is not better than you, and it could have a few weak points. What else can you accomplish?

Never put too much on your plate at one time. Always give yourself time to get things done if something goes wrong or you get tired. Take your time when doing good works. The enemy will believe sabotage will work against, but your positive works will succeed. When you believe something is going to work, think of ways it can function properly and work better. That's how most people get ideas.

Smaller ideas that tie into one another can help things along. If there are no flaws in the design of the cage, don't give up. You already developed the concept and said you can be free in your mind. Focus on the door—even if it doesn't work. Focus on those who know you are not free, and they can set you free. Hope is the most important thing when it comes to anything the mind can conceive. Never lose sight of that in good times or bad.

IF YOU LOVE YOURSELF, EVERYTHING YOU DO WILL WORK

The more energy you put into your craft or specialty, the more things will come back to you. First of all, you must believe in energy. Energy is all around us. My thoughts, the ideas, the ink, the paper, the people involved in this book all came from energy. If you're an astronaut in space, you might get chance to see a shooting star. If you like cars, you might see the most amazing vehicle in a high-speed race. While scuba diving, you might see a blue whale or a white whale. It's all about the energy you give toward that which you love most and the thoughts you put into it.

The goal of success is what you're going after. When you love something, you are fully committed to it. The love and affection you share with your craft is the force that drives your passion. When you walk into a bathroom, you expect the toilet to be clean. When you get in the elevator, the last thing you expect is the elevator to be jammed. The people who are responsible take their jobs seriously.

The job will be completed with love, care, time, and energy. The individual responsible for the job will put effort into the product you're using. Some people are lazy, but you're not like that. Love what you do for people at all times.

IF YOU THINK YOU'RE GOING TO LOSE YOUR MONEY, DON'T PART WITH IT

Picture yourself at the base of a waterfall, and a stream is running smoothly. When it gets closer to the waterfall, the stream becomes more rapid and unstable. While walking toward the water, you have a bucket. Where is it convenient to fill this bucket—in the waterfall, the rapids, or farther downstream where the waters are calm? At what point is it safe to build a dam to channel some of the water? When things are calm again, it's safe to enter the water. The stillness of the water offers you a chance to spot predators.

You need to apply this same methodology to business ventures. Your bucket is your way of life. Do you want to jeopardize that by miscalculating when to approach the stream? The stream is the revenue generated by the business. At the beginning, the water can be dangerous and unstable. The stillness can present hiding spots for predators. Always consider the risks of obtaining a new revenue stream. Do you want the waters to wash you away and carry that bucket away?

IF YOU WANT ANYTHING SAID, ASK A MAN—IF YOU WANT ANYTHING DONE, ASK A WOMAN

Some things are done best by men. Some things are done best by women. A busy man or woman can do a task quickly because they are already so busy that they'll knock it out with haste. Women take a task and do it with accuracy and precision. Women can be more compromising if you handle them with care. Men might put in a good word with the proper channels.

Think of them as lions and lionesses. You leave the light work for the females and the big tasks to the males. It all depends on the situation. This gives both sides credibility in their own respective positions. Assess what you seek from each individual—and use finesse to achieve your goal. Make sure you treat everybody equally.

When you cross paths with a woman, she arrived there before you did. In a male-dominated world, a woman has to use what she can to maneuver ahead. Communication allows them to detect bullshit in the bigger picture. Bullshit might disrupt the balance of success and progression. Women are quick to notice the bad apple in the group. This is a friendly suggestion to keep everyone cohesive. Have you noticed that a lot of the females in the animal kingdom are the most dangerous? There's a reason for that. Take note and respect all those you come across.

IF YOU WANT TO SEE HOW PEOPLE FEEL TOWARD YOU, FALSIFY YOUR SUCCESS

The easiest time to discover who is not in your favor is right at the beginning. Staff, friends, and family will be aware of your progress. Once a person finds out, everybody else will too. That is the way things work. This will work out in your favor because the second something new about you appears, people will notice. They will discuss everything you say and do. Most of them will not approve of things you do if they don't benefit them.

It is always best to keep everything you've done under wraps. Defending yourself against people who have nothing to do with themselves will never work out. You can easily spot someone who shouldn't be around by lying about your success. When people can't get an exact spot on your location, they try to recreate your image by falsifying information.

If you were abducted by aliens, the aliens might reveal how untrustworthy your friends are. You didn't go anywhere. You didn't do anything. You became invisible to people while hovering in the sky. What do people say about you? You should already have a clue. What are some of the things they believe happened to you?

You only vanished, but you didn't go anywhere. These premonitions are good indicators of future problems. You can stoke a fire by telling one person something and seeing how it gets back to you. Don't play people against one another, but if a little information causes certain people to talk, get away from them immediately.

IGNORE YOUR GUT—AND IGNORE YOUR LUCK

Ignoring your inner feelings is ignoring a voice from above. Not getting into much religion, there is energy and force that runs all that we know. Our instincts come from a long line of ancestors. Is it a coincidence that the benefits of the mind are exponential? The feelings we get accumulated from millennia of troubles and triumphs.

Humans have come a long way, and it's no wonder we haven't gone much further. Sometimes you are presented with an opportunity to do something much greater than you intended. You will know when the opportunity arises because what you planned to do with a simple idea will spiral into something you can't control on your own.

A boardroom is like a jungle. Feelings of predation strike at you as if you were in a jungle. These primal instincts come in handy during times of stress and frustration. Learn how to recognize what you feel, decipher your feelings, and let the situation play out. A good way to activate these feelings is to put yourself in a situation that will lead to excitement or rejection: asking a random person on a date, going to a business meeting, or setting up deals or meetings you can't handle.

Start small by asking someone for some change or to borrow their phone. Those emotional signals are your fight-or-flight responses. Who you are as person can change over time—but never ignore what you feel comfortable with.

Once you've mastered the recognition of these feelings, it's time to learn how people behave. Study some psychology or hang around different people. You will soon discover the environment is the reason for a person's behavior. Over time, you'll be able to predict what someone will do in their daily routines. If you know them, you'll see warnings of the coming dangers.

I'M NOT A RICH MAN—I'M A POOR MAN WITH MONEY

Money will make or break any relationship once it becomes large enough. Poor people are able to go from rags to riches because they know what it's like to lose everything. Think about getting on a treadmill sand running a mile. No matter how long you walk, you're not going anywhere. The second you get off, your legs feel strange. You didn't walk anywhere, you didn't leave the room, and you didn't see any new scenery.

Imagine running a mile on a track. You can run around the track and view different things while remaining in the same area. You get more of a workout, but the cost is time to arrive at the track, wear and tear on your shoes, and fatigue from running around the track.

You still haven't really gone anywhere, but you have exposed yourself to more of the outside world.

What if you run a mile in any direction? You don't know where you will end up. You don't know who you will see. You don't know what will happen. The first two scenarios seem better than before, and you know things can't get worse.

Rich people who have come from poor backgrounds know how to stretch their resources and save because they know what it is like to have nothing. They have come a long way, and the motivation and attentiveness to detail help them maintain a healthy, balanced lifestyle. They prevent themselves from going back to the way things were before.

No matter what happens under your feet or before your eyes, it should not change you as a person. Keep the same attitude you had before the success and keep yourself from losing it. There shouldn't be much that changes about you unless your life calls for drastic measures.

IN BUSINESS CONVERSATIONS, TIME, SPEED, AND RESOURCES ARE EXCHANGED

Everyone has something to offer, and the least fortunate person can offer you a bit of wisdom. In business, the most common thing you can trade is time. How much time and effort can you save if you join forces? Resources can always be found elsewhere. Locating, pricing, and testing can cut the number of resources offered. Your goal should be to save time and resources. The more you save, the more it frees up the ability to do bigger and better things.

With a foundation of trust, you can save precious time. You are proving you are worth the trust it takes to accomplish certain goals. The fruits of your ambitions and dreams will come to harvest in much more bountiful quantities after your labor.

INFLUENCE

Powerful people use influence to move other people. When trying to control your influence, imagine yourself in a stadium with everyone watching you. Picture people are far as the eye can see— and then imagine that everybody in the stadium is gray and colorless. Whenever you say something, the crowd changes colors from gray to red or blue. As the colors change, they spread like a wave.

Each time something occurs on the stage, the crowd changes color. The crowd can be affected by negative input and change to the color you like the least. It is up to you to make sure the people change color in your favor. Each time the color shifts, it goes along with the attitude of everyone watching.

The more attention you get, the greater the risk of everyone watching you at the wrong time. It is important that every person can see the best part of you. Once you obtain control, you should be able to jump in the crowd, turn your back on the stage, and be aware of what's going on in the crowd.

Like throwing small rocks into a pond, you want as many ripples as possible. You are keeping a steady flow of attention in people— unlike most individuals who throw big rocks in the pond to create massive amounts of attention. Your technique is consistency. The longer you hold people's attention, the more you build their interest. Try to grab everyone's concern on a deeper level—and do not fall prey to the harsh judgment of being different. No one can be louder than the roar of the crowd, and once they scream your name, keep them saying it over and over.

INNER COMIC

You should be okay with who you are as a person. Sometimes you wear the same thing every day and have less than most people. Think of it as being in a comic. Does the main character change clothes every day? The answer is no. It only happens with an upgrade in a new season. Do you see the main character changing his or her appearance?

The way you present yourself should stand out. Expand on your favorite comfort clothing, pajamas, or suits. If you like track suits, pick a color or two. Know what you are good at and what you are not good at. There is no perfect comic book character. Figure out what you want to master—and stick with it. You have more than one capability. You're the best at one specific thing. Be okay with being in your own skin. Be okay with a small, medium, or large build. Above all, don't let your enemies get you out of character.

IN ORDER TO KICK ASS, LIFT UP YOUR FOOT FIRST

Whatever your goal, get started immediately. Write down your minimum needs. You might have to annihilate to opposition. Keep going. A shovel doesn't care what's in front of it—and neither should you.

This book was created one word at a time. All it takes is one step. The first few steps will be the hardest, but once you establish the path and direction you want, go for it. You cannot afford to not live up to your full potential. Kicking ass might mean learning the hard way not to play around. If that is the case, so be it. Don't be gentle toward anyone who gets in your way to the top. No matter who it is. If they try to play you, let them have it. When you let them have it, give it everything you've got.

The next time somebody tries to play a game with you, they will think twice. When a task presents itself, take it. With any goal, you must go especially hard until the end.

INSPIRATION WITH NO ACTION IS MERELY ENTERTAINMENT

Everything you say, think, and do should revolve around your business, personal life, and success. That is how some of the most brilliant ideas have been created. They were focused on the task at hand and would not look away.

In the Trojan War, Odysseus thought of creating a giant horse out of the wood of the ships. If it was a gift, it would be received without hesitation. There was some risk involved because they could have easily burned the horse and saved themselves so much trouble. You should always approach your ideas and concepts by thinking outside of the box. Think of something you like and how it relates to your ambitions, find similarities, and try to mix them.

Creativity is the key to all permanent success, and you will learn how it lacks in other people. When you get inspired by something that is an indication that maybe it will fit in with your character. Don't fight the urge to do something greater than what you are doing now, at the expense of who you are right now. Everything changes over time and your personality, and character is no different.

INTEGRITY

Integrity is the quality of being honest, having strong moral principles, and being whole and undivided. When you speak, you are what you say. People only have two things in this world: their words and their lives. What you say will ultimately be to your satisfaction or your peril. Understand words mean nothing without mixing them the right way. Like a good beverage, it takes the right mixture at the right temperature to be refreshing to the body. The same goes with your words. Unless you say one word at a time, you need to know how to mix and match your words for your audience.

Words are nothing more than pieces of sound bent a certain way in the right frequency, pitch, and volume. We value the actions that come behind them. If someone says, "I'm going to the bathroom," you would think they were going to the bathroom. The communication is not in the words but in the actions.

The compromise of integrity and communication is the act of speaking before and after an action is carried out. Words are nothing more than permission slips for the action that follows.

IT'S BETTER TO BE TRUSTED THAN LIKED

In your climb to success, no one is really going to like you—and you shouldn't expect them to. Always do your job—no matter the cost. To be trustworthy is to be dependable. It's that simple. Anybody can say, "I don't like him or her."

There is nothing to worry about if you are a person of principles and morals. The rest will fall into place. People won't like you all the time. To be liked by everyone is to be deceived by everyone. If that isn't good enough for the people around you, then it never will be. Don't force it. If they can count on you to do the job, they will put up with things about you they don't like.

Trust is a two-way street, and if you can't trust the company you are around, there is no need to try to gain their trust. You don't have to like someone for them to do their job. When you gain the trust of people, it is a sign of acceptance.

IT'S EASIER TO SUCCEED THAN FAIL

It is a relief when you do something you've always wanted to do, especially the first time it comes to mind. That is true success. Even an attempt will always be better than letting the opportunity go by. It's like scratching an itch that has been bothering you. When you try to get to a spot you can't reach, the motion will cause a bit of comfort. It is the same concept for an action toward success.

The motion and process will do more for you than sitting around and letting time go by. You will never feel comfortable with yourself if you let dreams dissolve without putting effort into getting things done. Success is easier than failing because you never fail at something you do unless you quit.

Doubt and fear are the two main killers of dreams. Don't let failing plague your mind. Don't hang around anyone who can fill your head with bad thoughts. A rocket starts from ground zero. The thrusters help the space shuttle break the atmosphere and enter space. Find people who are like thrusters and help you get where you need to be. Enjoy the journey. Don't forget why you did it in the first place. Have more fun in your life. If it doesn't make you laugh, go back and figure out what the deal is.

IT'S NOT WHAT A MAN KNOWS

People will say a whole bunch of bullshit behind your back. That is just a way of life. The problem is when others start to believe it. If untrustworthy people believe anything they hear they should not be regarded as friends. When people know the truth and won't speak up, that is the same as agreeing with somebody's bullshit.

You can tell a lot about a person by how fast they learn the truth and what they do with it. The most underhanded and deceitful thing is to know the truth. Hear a lie, and then twist the truth so it coincides with the lie. Things like this rarely happen, but when they do, you have to be cautious. People who know the truth about you might have to defend you when they come across deception, but if they have some type of concern, they will defend you by stating what is true and what is not. It's that simple.

In some middle schools, the teacher might introduce a game that involves passing along a message. The teacher will give a message to pass along from one end of the classroom to the other. The message is changed and altered multiple times. You can be talking about apples, and the conversation ends up talking about oranges. It is a great way to learn how deceptive the mind and people can be when passing along messages. Never fall prey to the words of others. Like all creations, information, food, and resources, things can be filtered and tainted if they are processed long enough before ingestion.

INTRUSION

An intrusion is an unwelcome visit or interruption on privacy. At some point, you will become so much of a threat that someone will try to stop you from succeeding. They will breach your defenses via bribery, deception, or force. Do not let it get to you.

Only fools trust their enemies. They have no respect for you and will sabotage your growth for their gain. You can't let people like that drive you to the point you don't even trust the safety of your own walls. Do what is necessary to drive people like that out and move on to bigger and better things.

The sky is the limit, and when people take the time out to see what you have going on, they are threatened. When an intruder is detected, you don't destroy them immediately. You discover what has their attention before you remove that element to keep them from coming back. Double your defenses, remove the bait, and set a trap to see what their true mission is. They will never quit. They will come back over and over again until they destroy you or have what they seek. Get over it. You are in the big leagues now, and you need to tighten your security immediately. You are on the right path when things like this occur. It's a good sign that you're onto something.

KARMA

Karma is the sum of a person's actions in this state of existence—and previous ones—that decides a person's fate in future existences. You get in what you put out. If all you do is push negativity and be mean to people, you're going to receive negativity. Karma is like throwing a ball around the world and thinking it won't come back to hit you. Karma is a fascinating subject because everybody has it. What you do on your own time is developing your energy. If you go around sleeping with countless woman and talking badly about people, it is going to come back to you. What if one of those girls tries to set you up?

The best thing to do when you don't like someone is ignore them. Using people to get back at someone is bad. It leaves the door open for someone to intervene. When you hurt people repeatedly and think nothing will come about it, negative energy will poison the spirit of what you care about most. They are liable for dangers and other threats you leave behind.

Everyone is not built for the life you live. Be careful how you treat others. Karma works for good and for bad. Choose what you do carefully because it will come back in the actions and dealings of others around you.

KEEP YOUR LIFE A SECRET

One of the most important rules is knowing how much information someone has. The best way to stay above ground and not drown in your own misery or sorrow is to not tell anybody anything pertaining to your personal life, your business, or anything you have going on for yourself. Your information is the most important thing in your life.

The more people know your business, the more they know how to attack you. So much trouble can start when another person's bullshit infects your progress. Don't tell anybody anything. It can save you a major headache. It doesn't matter if it's good or bad—keep it to yourself. Only share on a need-to-know basis. I can't tell you how much drama I've been with people trying to take things from me or using information they believe is accurate as a weapon to tear me down. Save yourself. Imagine everyone has a gun on you. Giving them information is like giving them ammunition.

KEEP THE ENGINES RUNNING

When you step into a new situation, always keeping the engine running. Only put one foot in the door—and peek at any new opportunity before going for any type of reward. You never know what is lurking on the other side of an opportunity. Like all choices, once you start, it might be the only time to not follow through with a decision.

Do not trust yourself completely when doing any favors for yourself. You are the only one who can help yourself, and you are the only one stopping you. If you hurt yourself, the game is over. Having at least one person in your corner will a great benefit. They might have to rescue you from yourself.

The worst kind of defeat is one you give yourself. Don't proceed anywhere with a quick getaway plan. It is easier to interact with people when you know you can leave at a moment's notice. Never get into any situation that you can't back out of. Socializing with people will become a burden as you get older. It's important to practice good habits. Know who to interact with and who to stay away from. You are going to start craving attention soon. Try to impress people and demonstrate tenacity. Outside of business, always take situations at face value. Keep your getaway plan prepared, keep your protection secure, and keep your eye on the prize. People come and go. Don't get caught up in what they can give you. It's okay to make a business decision and attempt to repair any damages, but it takes discipline to escape the wrong crowd.

KNOW THE SELF OR BE CONQUERED BY THE SELF

Your biggest enemy is going to be temptation. You can have what you want, but it will take over your mind if you don't know how to handle it. As you grow, a lot of things that once were not attractive to you will become attractive. Things you once did not want to eat will suddenly become something you crave. That is how life works.

You better get control of yourself before you put yourself in a situation you can't handle. Maybe you should try introducing yourself to something new on a daily basis. Trying out new foods, meeting new people, and exposing yourself to different things are the best ways to learn what you can handle. If you were on a diet you, you might be tempted to indulge.

Even on a cheat day, use mental blocks when no one is around to stop you from hurting yourself. Don't go near the action that will save you when no one else can.

LAYERS

Nothing stops on the first try, and nothing is built with one set of walls. In your quest to build something or attack or defend yourself, there are going to be trials and tribulations. The best thing to do when preparing you for it is to accept that they are going to keep coming. Instead stopping a problem completely, you must break down the issue first. If it is thievery, the best defense is layers of defense.

A door to a house is a good defense because it provides a breaking point for the first assault of your home. With a phone or computer, it's better to put together a defense that is built like an onion. Each time someone breaks down a level of your defense, they lose momentum. They will slow down completely to get through you defense. On the other hand, an attack made of waves is better than sending all your forces at once since they could possibly be wiped out. Sending waves to break down the forces of an enemy works. Everything is built in layers, especially people. Use the first layer to lead you to the second layer and so on.

Pay attention to people's armor. Find a crack and begin digging. You will do more damage. If you leave a door unlocked, you store certain items or bring them with you. Simple gestures will save you the headaches of sabotage and deception when your back is turned.

LAZINESS

Everyone has laziness, and everyone suffers from it. The key to success is learning how to control it. The richest people are the laziest. They have others do the work for them, and then they take the credit. A good leader or boss would know how to do it with grace.

There will be days when you need a break, and those are the days to provide yourself with a break. Avoid doing work for the day. It's okay to write down a few ideas, but completely step away from your work and projects for a while. Give yourself at least one day a week to take a break. Provide yourself with one day a month of nothing. Completely dedicate it to leisure, pleasure, joy, happiness, and good old-fashioned fun.

Don't be ashamed of yourself if you crash one day. Every once in a while, it's okay to say, "Fuck it." That is a healthy mental attitude. It's possible to become sick of yourself sometimes. Nobody is above getting away from. The person in the mirror is with you 24/7. You might want a break from yourself every once in a while. It is possible to love yourself too much. Remember to give yourself time to heal— in all portions of your existence. Don't have too much work, too much stress, too much frustration, too much fun, or too much you.

LEADERS ARE LEARNERS

The best leaders are the best learners. They know exactly how to get a job done because they go about completing tasks according to the demands of the environment. They want to build toward the overall dream, but instead of taking a normal route, they change course and take detours. They stop along the way to learn the ins and outs of problems.

Anybody can be a great learner. You don't have to be in a position of command to learn from people. The best way to learn anything is at ground level. The most knowledgeable sources come from the underground because they collect the dirt that gets left behind from dirty, corrupt individuals. If you want information, ask somebody who has nothing to lose.

The answer you receive from one person might be different from another because of their circumstances or the way they feel toward the powers that be. That is why you learn from everyone around you. It's like talking to the owner of a company—sometimes the employees will tell you better. Everything is held by gravity, and everything held by gravity travels along the earth. Keep your ear to the earth.

LEAD WITH YOUR MIND

Act as if you have an arrow on your forehead. You have to put your shirts on a certain way, you have to walk through doors a certain way, and you have to maneuver through people a certain way. It's as easy as keeping thoughts like that in mind when you awake and begin the day. You have to be cautious before conducting any activities with a large instrument on your head. Every move, gesture, and step must keep that arrow from bending or hurting someone around you.

You must do the same thing with your mind as the thoughts thought go in and out of it. Your thoughts can make or break you and those you care about. Stepping toward someone the wrong way can lead to them being hurt. Always be careful of the mind-set you since it affects the safety and structure of whatever you create.

Always pay attention to those who try to break your arrow. They will put you in situations that force you to move uncontrollably. You can keep track of your positioning, and then it's over. Don't dull yourself with shortcomings and mistakes made from not being prepared.

LEARNING

Learning is the acquisition of knowledge or skills through experience, study, or by being taught. Learning involves being able to evolve. You can't be the same person and learn different things at the same time. You learn what a car is, but once you actually drive one, you can do what is necessary to perfect the physical portion of driving.

Learning requires you to reflect on new information. It requires learning to take notes and rewriting them. You also need feedback. Feedback is important because it offers information from a different perspective. Fail twice as much as you succeed to cut the learning curve. Observe those who are doing what you want and emulate them. Create mind maps for your thoughts and ideas. Take notes of your notes.

When you finish writing down information, rewrite the notes with more precise detail—and repeat until you have a third of what you started with. Learn and study with your favorite sense. If listening to music is one of your favorite activities, listen to audiobooks. If you like to draw, create mind maps for your ideas. If visuals are how you learn, create one-minute videos on a subject.

Experience seems like a good idea. Step out there and see what you can do. Whatever you like to do most is how you should study because the information is digested smoother that way. Never stop learning. Become a learning machine—even for useless information—because you will discover that information is not useless. It can generate wealth and success.

LEGACY IS MORE IMPORTANT THAN CURRENCY

Why would you want to chase money when you can have so much more through time? Your goal should be leaving behind something your kids can give to their kids. That's not to say that money is not important and holds no value, but you should be building something that requires maintenance and care for the present and the future. Always keep in the back of your mind what you can leave for others. You never want your family to be empty-handed. If you don't have a family, choose someone who is close to your heart.

You could leave something behind for your city or village. Concentrate on the future and start building toward it immediately. Any mistakes you make along the way are pieces to a much bigger prize. A legacy speaks volumes about a person when money can't. In reality, if you are working toward a legacy, someone will profit from the venture. If not, you need to rethink what you are doing. If it doesn't make you any money, you shouldn't be doing it. Don't make it a priority.

Build for the future. Leave behind everything that doesn't contribute to your goals and dreams. You are always on the move because time is progressing. You are on a ship that never stops moving. You can't worry about who or what you lose on the way to your destination. People might betray you, jump ship, or try to sink the ship by letting on water.

LEFT AND RIGHT

There are two sides to every story. We have two ways of thinking about things. There are two sides of thought processes. With one personality for work and one personality for recreation, both should make up one person. In each mind-set, there should be a world that consists of mental stimulations and physical stimulations to help you remain stable.

Try to keep one mind-set from leaking into another one. You need to keep both lives separate. If you have hobbies, you might not have two different mind-sets. Most people live two different ways and don't even realize it. Some rap artists come from rough backgrounds but change into artists. They didn't reach their potential until after growing into what their environment wanted. That doesn't have to be you. If you realize you like more than one thing, you can be more than one person.

You don't have to be two different people. If you are good at more than one thing, you should have something to balance out the chaos. You can't get much done if you always focus on the same things. You have to give your mind time to think and process other ideas. Find an activity to help you with your creativity. Lawyers sometimes play poker to learn how to read people's faces better. Find something you like to do besides working that offers some creative space.

LESSONS

Everything is a lesson in life. Everything you go through on a daily basis—good or bad, small or large, big or tall—is a lesson to be learned. Even if you sit in a room the entire day and do nothing, you learn not to sit in a room for too long.

When it comes to lessons, you definitely want to learn one every day. You won't remember the majority, but you will remember the most important ones and the experiences they gave you. After a certain age, life gets repetitive. The best way to avoid unwanted repetition is to avoid making the same mistakes. The same pitfalls will approach you if you are not prepared, and the same people who want you to fail will reappear in different forms.

Life is one big lesson, and it has no mercy. Take pride in your walk of life and respect the ideas you need to be aware to survive. Every day is a lesson you can learn from. Plan a strategy for the day and grade yourself on how it played out. You don't have to be harsh. Just be firm, acknowledge the turns, and avoid failing. This is an everyday routine. Learning will put you ahead. If the task requires a left instead of a right, the execution does not have to be perfect.

LET PEOPLE DO THE LEGWORK FOR YOU

You can be copied, plagiarized, or imitated. Your works will be stolen. Sometimes it works in your favor because you want the message to be sent about who you are and what your name is. In business, the key to success is advertising and marketing. If it's free, why deny it? You want all your ducks in order. When it is time to take back what you own, you can be precise.

In war, it is not the best offense that wins. It is the best defense. If you know what your opponent will do and how they think, you will never lose. Most assaults follow a pattern—even when people are trying to take something from you. They will not stop until they have it.

Let them do all the work, the heavy lifting, the procedures, and the processes. Eliminate them and take what is yours. This breaking and entering your dreams will not be tolerated. That's like moving into someone's house without their permission and installing furniture and other belongings. Eliminate them without mercy.

LET THEM FIGHT

In order to survive, don't try to consume all the glory in every battle. Some people like to prove themselves. If you take all the glory, there is going to be conflict. Be kind to those who want to get their hands dirty. When trying to protect you, think about your future. People will also try to gain glory from your defeat. It is important to let the small parties clash. Don't get involved in any conflict you didn't start. You gain additional favor when they take on battles in your name and gain victories. They gain strength, and you gain merit.

Avoid as many fights as possible. You can lead from the back or the front. During wars, let them fight. Some losses might occur, but that is not important. Your survival and the legacy you are building are important. Step back from time to time and let others handle a few conflicts. It's not selfish to let others do some of your dirty work.

Don't take away someone's ability to prove themselves to you. Even if it's just once, it will mean the world to your supporters. Your ambitions and passions are golden for the person who gives them life. Each and every person who takes your hand on the journey looks at you in a different way. Step back sometimes. You can't control people. Let them make some decisions on your behalf. Not all will be promising— but nothing is.

LET YOUR ACTIONS SPEAK FOR YOU

Don't try to argue or negotiate with people. Just sit back and let the magic flow from your fingers. Never try to convince anyone what your message is trying to convey. Speak through the actions and steps you take to secure your role and position. If certain individuals are not convinced, it's not in your best interests to try to appease them.

Speaking will do nothing for you but lead you into temptations and actions you don't need. Avoid speaking too much because it will do you no good. Everyone has a mouth. Everyone can speak. How many people do what they say after they say it? That is the difference between being heard and being listened to.

Instead of going through the trouble of delivering a message, carry the goal that comes from it. Explain why you did something in the first place. Demonstrate things more than once— three times at most. If you are doubted after demonstrating your actions three times, get away from the area. People are looking for you to fail, and your words and actions are falling on blind eyes and deaf ears.

LEVEL 3

Level 3 is the point of no return. You have mastered everything there is to know about a subject, topic, training, or practice. The best of the best is when somebody does a super combo on you and fails. You never fail or lose out on anything. When it goes down, you never miss a beat.

To be Level 3 is to be on top of your game. No ifs, ands, or buts. To be that person is to also know the ins and outs of what you perfect. If you run fast enough, you can dodge time itself and move into the future. If you strong enough, you can jump so high it seems like you're flying.

Level 3 is the peak of your potential. You can do extraordinary things. Respect for yourself before any potential is desired. You have to keep the mind and body in tip-top shape. The best athletes know about nutrition and working out. A marksman knows how to read the weather to get the exact curvature of a round. He usually has a spotter, but perfection is of the utmost importance.

One soldier on a mission can change everything. He or she needs no assistance with anything and is more than willing to share the hard work and rewards. Strive to be the best there is in a field. You will look like you're flying, but you have talents beyond compare. The best is an insult to you. Work on it until you know more than others and can deceive them by pretending to be stupid. You can position people because you have figured out the puzzle of perfection.

LIFE HAS NO MIDDLEMAN

Everybody wants to be in the middle of something. They always want to get right into the middle of what you want. You can't even get a drink of water without hoping the sink comes through for you. Life has no middleman. You can't do what you want on your own. Going directly to the source doesn't mean a mountain of product, and it doesn't necessarily mean being a high-ranking official. It means the rewards and benefits of your hard work and labor include purity and hastiness in request. You get what you asked for in a timely fashion. The water from a faucet might come where you want it to come from, but the water gets contaminated in the pipe. It would be a lot less dirty in a stream. I wouldn't trust a camera, photo, or words from anyone because they are the middlemen to the answers I seek. In order to get medication, you have to contact a doctor for a prescription. The middleman is kind of like the ferry between you and the destination. Shorten the lines between you and everything you want.

LIFT EVERY VOICE

Raise your hands, say, "Hear me," and find the inner spirit that says, "I can do anything." Scream like you've never screamed before. Scream loud in your innermost thoughts. Imagine expressing yourself so loudly that the earth is shaking, glass is shattering, and tornadoes are forming. It's as if the world is tearing itself apart.

With your head raised, use the confidence this voice brings you. Joining plenty of groups makes you feel unique, important, and appreciated. Be sure to link yourself to a lot of social media channels that will broadcast the best parts of you when you're not paying attention. This is an investment on your behalf. This task does not have an indefinite time limit. You might be reaching out to people for years before your effort is returned. You want as many people as possible to hear and know exactly who you are.

The times of deception and sabotage will be easier to pass through with more mouths speaking highly of you. Be sure to communicate with people who will remember you and protect you in the future. Those people will offer you opportunities for positive exposure.

LITTLE BY LITTLE

Little by little, anything can get done—from the tallest building to the smallest painting. If you put your mind to it, you can accomplish anything. The best way to go about your day is to along at least five things you want to get done. Break it down for your daily routine. If you are building a house, car, or rocket ship, start where it matters the most. Put a tire on, put a window in, and plot the course of the rocket. The next day, do more of the same thing. Before you know it, you will be on your way.

The key is to set a strict schedule and stick to it. The house might be put together, the car might be running, but the rocket ship is still not completed. That's fine. Finish a task and leave it alone— even if you want to do some extra work. Don't go any further than the schedule you set for the day. If you really want to get ahead, schedule another set of tasks. You will tire at first, but the urge to get ahead will be greater than the urge to stop. That is when to set up some control measures. The biggest interference is outside influence. Paying attention to other people will cause you to stop too early. When you are finished, leave it alone. Don't respond to people who try to slow you down.

LOVE PEOPLE AND USE MONEY—DON'T LOVE MONEY AND USE PEOPLE

People are the cause of a lot of benefits and issues. Before making any decisions, you should assess who is going to be involved. Nine times out of ten, somebody in your party is best for the scenario. It is up to you to decide who that person is.

If all you are doing is chasing money, you are in for failure. Imagine money being a stream. Imagine your friends, associates, and co-workers looking for the stream. Which one of them has a good nose, good eyes, or good ears? Let people assist you with things they are good at. Do you care more about them or quenching your thirst? Do you care more about your support or the water? Everybody needs water. Don't become so obsessed with finding your goal that you disregard the important people in your life.

MAGNETISM

Everyone is attracted to something. Below the surface, you might find yourself attracted to many different things and many different people. A wise individual wouldn't ignore the signs. You can learn a lot from interacting with things outside your norm. Explore more. Live a little. This is not about making new friends or seeing new things. This is about your comfort level.

Most people can detect whether they want to be around you. Something inside of us gives it away. Sometimes we want to escape ourselves and go to a more comforting location. If you get in trouble with your parents or superiors, you want to leave. Someone close to you can detect that energy. Your attitude, tone, and body language can remain dormant. It is good to stay adjusted and secure within yourself most of the time so people don't say you have bad vibes or feel uncomfortable around you. In reality, your mind is trying to escape your body and push other people's thoughts and feelings toward you.

MANIPULATION

Manipulation is the act of convincing or coercing something or someone in a skillful manner or a clever or unscrupulous way. You have to smile a little bit or dance to get them to drop their guard. Manipulating people is wrong and immoral, but it can be a necessity. How else would you convince someone to work for you and perform excellently? A little deception is healthy, and it helps people do what they are told. You can be stern and firm with everyone you meet all the time, but it's going to take a little bit of this and a little bit of that to make people like you.

Share in the wealth, show people some good spirit, and give them a show for their money. Put on your best superhero mask, get in front of whoever you need to convince, and get the job done. The easiest way to get anyone to like you is to be a good speaker. Master the art of communicating and speaking to people. That is the best route if you don't want to make someone conduct the same behaviors on you. Connecting to people isn't as hard as it seems. Find similarities and use them to get to know people.

MASTERS AND MENTORS

A good student takes notes on everything. A master possesses a substantial amount of knowledge about a specific subject. A person who is trying to copy can provide an alternate route to a goal. The dumbass wants to copy you. Use them to see what can go wrong. Find a professional to teach you the ins and outs. A wise man is capable of passing down lessons. Think of how fast you can learn from the mistakes of someone else and keep your record clean. When seeking a mentor, look for someone who does exceptionally well in whatever you are trying to master. Look at the evolution of your skills. A mentor is there to help you stay on track. Do not waste their time with useless data. A mentor should only be there when you have something you can't figure out. Take notes, be respectful, ask plenty of questions, and put the lessons to good use.

MAKING A LIVING

The quickest way to get to the top is to help others. When helping others becomes a habit, you help when help is needed. If you keep leading people to the water to drink, one of them eventually will ask if you know how to use the water for other means. Did you know you can use water to make electricity?

Doing reconnaissance for others will never get tiresome if you are doing it solely to help. It's going to lead you to valuable information. Be patient with yourself while others are being nourished because you are building a foundation of trust. The people you help today could help you tomorrow. People might think that is bribery or deception. Why not pay it forward and continue your progress while sharing the wealth?

Knowledge can be shared through the ears and eyes. Lead by example, show people the things they need to do to be successful, and provide a friendly ear and a helpful word. Even if you never make it, someone is going to come back for you. That water you led them to might have been a life-saving source of energy. They might thank you later with a position or a check.

MEASURE TWICE AND CUT ONCE

To measure twice is to make sure the outcome goes as expected. Nothing is ever perfect, but measuring something thoroughly and accurately is the best way to go when figuring out problems and details. Measuring doesn't mean taking a ruler and checking the distance of something all the time.

Taking account of all the variables is important when trying to deduce whether something can go wrong. It's not enough to say, "I've got this." It takes discipline to know everything that can go right or wrong. Before you execute a plan, consider every last variable. The mind is important, and underestimating someone can be detrimental to your plan. To avoid failure, set aside some extra time to make room for failed attempts. Take a minute to make a plan C—and go from there.

MENTALITY

People with many material things seem to obtain more with ease. They repeatedly get things that shouldn't be acquired so easily. It's not because they are better than you. It's not because they are smarter. They applied their mind to what they wanted and gave it to themselves. For those who inherited money, a friend or family member gave it to them. You might receive a pair of shoes, a car, or a house. Once you acquire those things, you might wonder about more. You need a belt to go with those shoes or a car to go with that house. You need rims to put on that car or a new engine. You are focused on an upgrade because you can see, hear, and touch the object you wanted so much.

Your mind is satisfied and ready to move on to the next challenge. With things you want, convince yourself that you already have them. Put on the outfit you want to go with those shoes, buy the mats you want to put in that car, visit the art designer you want to create your vision, or go to the dealership and touch the car. Visit a site where you want to construct a special house, building, or whatever is on your mind.

You have to stimulate the other senses to let the mind grow into the idea of you having what you desire. If you know what the car looks like, the leather smell gets in your nose. The paint will tell you what driving will be like for you. You can take a picture and place it on the steering wheel. The idea is to keep that dream alive and fuel it with all your energy. It starts with belief, it ends in the mind, and it is born into reality.

MIGHT AS WELL BE HAPPY

The hardest thing to do is let go. Let go of anything that ever made you question yourself. Be happy—no matter what. Be happy for your glory and your suffering. Things could be so much worse. When you discover something is wrong, it is only the beginning of what will occur if you don't deal with it. That doesn't mean you can face changes and new situations with an open heart and a smile. When you wake up, be happy about reentering the world. Be thankful for your sound mind and the thoughts that travel through your head.

Nobody is ever going to support you in the exact way you want them to. You might need to help them in their time of need. Being happy is free. All you have to do is be happy. If you find it hard to be happy, don't expect others to be happy with you. It all starts on the inside. If you can't manage yourself, how can you manage anyone else? Each day, look in the mirror and congratulate yourself for making it to another day. You need to hear supportive, kind words from yourself. Everyone needs support and love—even if you have to provide it for yourself.

MIND READER

To read someone's mind, you must have a clear head. Observe the entire context of what is going on. Who is involved? How are they involved? Why are they involved? What will they gain by sabotage? Will they receive something if the outcome goes in their favor? Who else is involved? How are they involved? What are they saying? What are they doing? When do they say it? When do they do it? What type of damage might occur?

Everyone has a motive. What is behind these moves he or she is making against you? What are the exact words being used? What is their reaction when you bring up problems? If it's more than one person, analyze the same data—and discover what they have in common. When you are attacked, you can distinguish the details of the assault by what it is based around. You don't necessarily understand this person. You might know the history of the people involved and how it causes them to behave.

People might tell you how to behave. Use their opinions as guidelines. Try filtering your movements through three people. Each perspective will help you. An enemy will react gladly about a bad situation, an associate will question what is going on, and a comrade or mentor will give you the benefit of the doubt and tell you how to fix it.

MIND YOUR AUDIENCE

Always be attentive to who you're in front of and who could be watching you at any moment. Someone is always watching you. When you become valued, the world will start to notice who you are. Keep a close eye on who is watching you. Make every move count. If no one is observing you at the moment, pretend they are. Eventually, spectators will pay attention to you.

What is the difference between a chef and a chemist? Nothing. They both mix and match other creations to present something new and exciting. A chef specializes in cooking, and a chemist specializes in science. A general and coach specialize in communication and keeping a team together.

People can relate to you and each other. Don't change who you are as a person. Instead, enhance your message. You are trying to convey your message to people. You will be tested and challenged, but that doesn't mean you lose your audience.

MINIMIZE PLANNING TO MAXIMIZE REVENUE

Jump in the game as soon as possible. There is no time for strategy or repairs. Just go for it. The best way to start any venture is through experience. You will learn more from experience than a book will ever teach you. Don't look for a guide to something you can learn on your own. Unless somebody offers you a helping hand, try to do things yourself. Hit the ground running.

Would you really seek help for something you like to do? When is the last time you looked inside a manual to learn how to play a video game? Go for what you know. The time is now. Go for it. Keep track of the new discoveries as you learn new things. When reading a book, try to discover as much as you can. You actually don't need anything to begin succeeding. All you have to do is start. You can grow, upgrade, and change your business format as you progress. The goal is to start receiving money quickly. Don't rip someone off—but begin your path to success. As that stream starts to flow, your income will grow. Figure out how to siphon it into bigger and better things. Change the way it flows. You can always come back to later to find out what is wrong with your venture. Get started today!

MIXING JOURNEYS

When someone doesn't listen to you, they might try to drag you into it. They might alter the outcome you have developed for yourself. Some people might take the same path as you—and then try to press their shortcomings on you. They are trying to live a life that doesn't belong to them. When it goes to shit, they will try to give it back to you. It is like a bad dream you cannot wake up from.

Knowing what you are interested in will prevent you from making mistakes. Being a master of your craft allows you to know the rules and understand the consequences of bad judgment and ill-advised actions. Jealousy leads to all types of dangerous, sporadic, unpredictable, unstable, and embarrassing behaviors. Most people will sit back and wait for you to fail, but if they can get a helping hand during the proceedings, they will.

Your enemies are like hungry animals waiting for anything you drop or leave behind. They want what you have. If these people decide to jump ship and start their own ventures, they will ask for assistance. Don't save them. Let your enemies do away with them and eliminate themselves. People who pretend to be you and use your name for their own selfish purposes should be regarded as enemies and be shown no mercy.

MOMENTUM AND MUSCLES

When you begin to do anything, you might stumble or fall, but you should keep going. After a while, you will hit your stride. This will happen if you begin doing something you have a passion for. If you switch from a small bicycle to a bigger one, you already have the proper training. You just have to learn how to control a bigger vehicle.

You are basing your existence around what you are trying to build. As you progress, you will learn that nothing can really stop you. It's not that you can't be stopped or won't be stopped—it's that you refuse to. After running, the body brings down the heart rate, blood pressure, and excitement level. It might make you feel awkward. Momentum is the ability to keep going. You should take pride in your progress and continue on in your struggle.

Muscles can be grown, and the atmosphere conditions them. The mind is a muscle, the body is a muscle, the spirit is a muscle, and thoughts are muscles. If you were asked to jump into a pool, your mind would trigger a defense mechanism. Your mind is doing calculations and coming up with data. These deductions come from mental strength. Spiritual muscles are telling you not to harm yourself.

Each portion of your existence has a limit, but it will heal and form a stronger bond within itself. The challenges are nothing in comparison to what you've already done for yourself. People, problems, and circumstances should not stop your progress. You have the strength to overcome any obstacles in your way.

MONEY PEOPLE

Many wealthy people believe everything has a price. Nothing in their lives is stable except their bank accounts. They thrive and run off of money and more money. Trust is limited in these people's lives, and they believe they can buy anything. Everyone has a price, and everything is for sale, but nothing is valuable.

Nothing remains the same, and nothing has the same value as the day before. Those people can offer some of the worst encounters because their friendship is based on the income you generate. Not all rich people are greedy, but many think they can overpower people with their money. Money, power, and respect are the only things they respect, but it's not entirely their fault. After being in business for so long, the mind becomes conditioned to thinking about profit and loss.

People immediately access the value you bring to the table. They should be regarded as allies in your inner circle. It is not wise to get too close to these people. A lot of insecurity arises from being so successful because they have to live up to your potential and can no longer display weakness in the eyes of their rivals.

Don't get caught up in the whirlwind of association with these people. Their concern for you is limited. Love and affection are required in any relationship, but you need to be careful not to mix money and pleasure with these individuals. Be as cordial as you can to maintain their respect and admiration—but watch yourself with wealthy people. Those people will try to surround you with their money. Be careful who you allow around you at such a high level.

MORE THAN ONE

There is more than one in everything. Only the unwise or foolish would think anything else. Never think there is only one way to do something. Keep your eyes and ears open for changes and opportunities. An incident might teach you about future endeavors that you might not see coming.

There are usually three damages that occur after a problem: the problem, the damage, and the effect. A flat tire on the way to work is damage to the car, makes you late for work, and is costly. The problems are always presented in threes. You have to figure out the purpose of the discovery. By applying this data to people, you can quickly figure out people's motives. With a fight in the lunchroom, the problem is a fight, the damage is a suspension, and the effect is socialism, grades, and influence. You will realize where the real threat is and what the true intentions of people are. Spread the ideas out on a map when analyzing the data of a person, place, or thing. It's not always what's in front you that is the interest. The outcome and impact determine the type of evolution.

MOTIVES

Everybody has motives, and you would be a fool to think otherwise. The best thing to do is use people for what they are good for. The most important thing is happiness, and sometimes that can hurt others. Stay in your own lane. If people want to follow you, they can—but if they can't help you, let them go. You shouldn't have any space for extras your bandwagon.

Pay attention to the reasons behind everyone's behavior. That's the definition of a motive. This book helps you become more aware of things like this. Check out everybody to see where their heads are. At any moment, things can change.

If somebody's end result doesn't vibe with you, don't join up with them. Trust plays a key role in who you allow around you.

MULTIPLY EVERY PURCHASE BY FIVE FOR FUTURE INVESTMENT RISKS

Life is a gamble, and throwing away your hard-earned is money is not worth it. Whenever you make a purchase, you should calculate the amount being charged. The value of a dollar often decreases. Twenty dollars doesn't go as far as it used to. Marketing, overhead, and shelf costs are not cheap. Think of the money you are spending every day as an investment.

Every dollar spent should encourage the growth and expansion of your dream. A bag of chips every now and then doesn't hurt, but buying expensive clothing or shoes is not a good choice. Don't let people convince you to make financial choices you might not agree with. A hobby or collection is a great way to spend a small amount of money on something you like or hold dear. If it appreciates in value, you can perhaps indulge yourself. The value of what you enjoy in material things should match your persona.

MYSTERY

Err on the side of caution, leave out everything, and allow people to think whatever they want. Don't give the public anything. There is a difference between public opinion and what one person thinks. A person is smart, but people are stupid. Don't bother with convincing people or one person. Let the crowd think whatever they want and leave as much as possible with the one person. They will come up with their own conclusions. The answer is always in front you.

Don't waste your time. Most people are attracted to mysteries. Play along with the stories people make up about you—if they benefit you. You want to be misunderstood and mistaken all the way up until you reveal what you want the world to know. Take enjoyment out of people never really knowing the real you. As you grow within yourself and do better, you should have a hard time keeping up with yourself. If you can outrun yourself, no one can ever catch up to any pursuit you set your mind to. You are moving so fast and exploring so much that your brain can't even process what you like anymore. When someone asks your favorite food or color, you should have an answer for that question. You experience a tremendous amount of new things, and it's hard to figure out what you like in the first place. Play games with yourself before anyone else. Have a bit of fun with who you see in the mirror. Always see the perfection in your reflection. That will the best friend you can depend on in the future.

NEGOTIATION

A negotiation is a discussion aimed at reaching an agreement. Within a negotiation, there are many different elements. Is it a win-win solution? A win-win solution leaves all parties satisfied with the outcome. Make sure the client has no resentment. When discussing terms, little decisions lead up to big ones. Instead of focusing on the big picture, use their resources to place the pieces in the right spots before going after the big picture. Aim for the no in the beginning of conversation. Take every objection as a question. A no establishes a boundary that must be addressed before moving on.

Try not to jump at the first offer. There is always a little more to get if you keep going. Always agree with people during a proposal. Do not argue. Instead of saying, "You're wrong," or "I disagree," say, "You're right. How can we fix this?" A negotiation usually means the person has something you want. Everybody you negotiate with has what you want. Someone is going to have what you want or know where to find it. Be prepared to look for those people.

Within every negotiation, a person will possess situation power, expertise power, reference power, and reward power. The reward could be a private jet, a villa, or other things of that nature. These are important principles and ideas to remember. Be wise in who you spend your time with.

NEVER BE EASILY TRIGGERED

Some people will flex on you for no reason. They insist that if you don't respond, it makes you weak. They say and do things to get you to jump and hang on every word that comes out of their mouths. The actions are blinding, and their tones are deafening. Don't you have something better to do? No. People like that don't have anything to do with their time and effort. They're trying to drag you down with them. It says a lot about a person who decides to antagonize someone who is beneath them. If you are so much better than me, why must you constantly try to prove it?

When someone tries to get you out of your comfort zone, it's always about things you want or want to do. Enemies might drive a car you want or hang around people you thought were worth chasing. In reality, they are trying to trigger you. Most of the time, it's to calculate your next move. If you react to a certain car, then they know you want to drive it. Now that they know you have an automobile interest, treacherous action will take place around cars. They might have certain people riding them in front of you or showing off in them. You have to ignore people like that and reverse the moves.

If you ride in a car that is less than presentable, remain humble and smile. They will have no choice but to move forward or be made. It is not that they have what you want—it's how you look better with it. The reaction gets them going. The less you react, the less they have to go on. Those people want to get a reaction out of you. Don't react. That sets them up to show their hands. Keep your emotions in check when dealing with the world. Most of the time, they are trying to get under your skin.

NEVER COMPLAIN OR EXPLAIN OTHER PEOPLE'S BEHAVIOR

Many people look at complaining as a weakness, and it is. To complain is to confess how a situation is hurting you. It causes your mind to falter. You have given up holding your ground psychologically and have resorted to releasing the tension verbally. Don't do this. All is not lost. Sometimes the things you want are going to take much more time and effort than you anticipated. That doesn't mean you should give up or cry. It means you are troubled and need to refocus on what is most important.

Don't think about what is going through another person's brain. Don't wander outside your own mind. No matter what you do for people, you will be betrayed by someone close to you. They will toss you to the side the second you reprimand them and don't do exactly what they want you to do. Don't let your charisma go to waste. Don't worry about how others handle themselves in times of crisis. That is not up to you to be concerned with. You need to concentrate on your goals, tasks, and objectives at all times.

Sometimes you can explain what someone else is doing and take the time to see what the problem is, but most of the time, it won't work like that. Don't ever say out loud what the problem is. Even if it really means something to you, don't let go of why you started in the first place. Everything has a cause, and strength begins on the inside.

NEVER CONSIDER THE CONCEPT OF FAILURE

Failure only happens when you stop or die. That's it. Most people's definition of failure is the timing of when something has to get done. If you don't do something exactly when you say you will and exactly how you say it, it counts as a failure. That is completely false. You should never count yourself as a failure. You are never a failure. You won the second you tried.

The problem is that many people can't take a setback. Your new outlook on failure should be the progress toward a goal and beginning a new journey. If you decide to come back one day, the game starts all over again. Failure doesn't exist, but it can take hold of your mind. Even if it takes you the rest of your life to do one task, it just took you longer than expected. You will fail to make steps along the way, but those mishaps are not failures.

The only way to not succeed is to let go of your dreams. You will require a shoulder to lean on and a source of faith when the going gets tough. Respect your strengths and weaknesses and learn to cope when you can.

Who you associate with will define your perception of what is acceptable and not acceptable. Those elements are out of your control. Pay attention. Those who really support you will never allow you to believe all is lost.

NEVER GO IT ALONE

Just like having network, you need a trusted team. You need a group of people who know how you think and which way you will go when the tide turns or if shit hits the fan. They are an extension of your intentions, and they know how you want things to be done without you being present. In addition to being capable of making business decisions without fear of blowback, losing money, or making mistakes, your team should have things in common with you. Everyone around you should be a reflection of your appearance, thoughts, dress, and everything it takes to remain cohesive as a unit. Nobody has to be perfect—or too special—but if they put on a uniform, you ought to be proud. Your team should be the best at their tasks. They should be capable of doing a perfect job—no matter what task is presented. If you were to venture off somewhere far away without any warning, your team should be able to run everything without you. The most important word to apply to everyone involved with you is *capable*. If they are capable, they are compatible.

NEVER INVEST IN SOMETHING YOU CAN'T DRAW WITH A CRAYON

Simplicity is essential when working toward a goal. A lot of times, we try to create a whole ecosystem behind a general idea. The key is to start small and grow into something much larger. At a restaurant opening, they don't have any specials or favored dishes because they don't have enough customer responses to know what people like.

When you are online, they switch to certain games and stick with them. People might subscribe to certain games over others. It's all about what the customer wants and what you can offer them. You might end up doing something you never thought you would do because of what people enjoy. It's best to keep an open ear. The most intelligent way to go about this is to create something from scratch. You can discuss it in one minute and draw it out on a napkin. You really don't know what your customers will like. It is best to start out small and grow. When you start from a simple place, you can understand people's perspectives.

NEVER TELL PEOPLE HOW YOU FEEL

In life, keep your emotions solid. Like a poker face, you should not be readable at first glance. The best way to keep your emotions in check is to check them at the door. Lie to yourself in the mirror if you have to—but keep things in perspective. Your mind has to be in tip-top shape. Do not disclose personal feelings to anyone—not even yourself. Pretend a camera and sound recorder are always on you. It might not be easy, but do not release your inner thoughts.

Take your time to find ways to release yourself with revealing too much. No matter what you say, it's never going to be taken the right way. Don't even go there. People might do stupid things to get a response out of you, and that is when you must tighten up the most. Even if somebody admits they are doing something to bother you, keep those thoughts to yourself and say okay. People are puzzle pieces, and whatever information and position you fill them with is how they will fit into the picture. They can destroy that picture if you are not careful.

NINE OUT OF TEN

When you come across any group of people, the first thing you want to do is find out who the smartest one is. Who has what? Who is doing what? Who is the leader? What is the focus of the group? And so on. Out of ten idiots, one of them is a genius. The point of this exercise is to understand that people like to play stupid. The smartest person tends to behave as if he or she is the dumbest. Once you discover how smart people really are, they can no longer sneak anything by you.

The key ingredient in any culture is a person who is smarter than he or she lets on. Usually, the smartest person in all settings is the one achieving the most with the least amount of effort. In almost all settings, the smartest person is collecting a serious percentage of the take from the whole group. That person will always dress, talk, and proceed in a highly sophisticated manner. Around everyone else, the group might have two who are high in stature and intelligence. This could include one person out in the open and one person hidden deep in the group. Even though one person might pretend he doesn't have the answers, he does. There can be an even worse individual hiding among everyone. That person might be watching for clues for how and when to control everyone else and not get caught. When you ask who is in charge, the main leader is nowhere to be found.

The real leader could be the first person you are introduced to, but he might lead you to his second-in-command. The leader hides in plain sight. You really never have to worry about being in situations like this unless you get high up in the food chain of a business or you're involved in a market that requires its leaders to remain hidden.

Be cautious when seeking the person in charge in any adventure. The leader wants to avoid any interference from the outside world. Be smart in your views, assessments, and analyses of people, groups, and associates. People who play stupid do not have the best intentions. Why wouldn't they share what they know in the first place to benefit everyone? This could be to protect everyone from the costs and penalties of being so high up, but more often than not, they are using the group as leverage.

OBSERVATION

Native Americans would watch animals eating certain herbs and drink from specific streams to discover their effects. When there is chaos, take a step back and observe what is going on. The best thing you can do is notice sudden changes in the scenery.

Minor details can harm the beauty of a situation. Pay attention to the way people behave around each other, their nature, and behavior toward themselves. It's free and helpful to be able to know information on a given topic without asking for it. When watching people, be sure to step all the way back from the situation. Do not participate in any situation you are watching. They must not feel your eyes on them.

ORCHESTRATION

If you have all your ducks in order, individuals may try to stop you from succeeding. They will do everything in their power to stop you. They will cross the line and sacrifice themselves to stop you. They will do the worst they can right in front you.

Recognize the motives, weapons, and tactics your enemies use. Don't get caught up in the confusion and mischief. Concentrate on what they want to stop. All types of plots and plans will be developed and executed if you are not careful. You have to see through the fog or mystery to see what's important. The orchestration will begin with people who are involved in your life and the roles they play.

Your enemies will try to keep in touch with each other as you shift your goals. Be careful.

PATIENCE AND PEACE

The best feeling is when you wake up. Even in the worst of times, those first ten minutes are full of peace and bliss. When you first awake, you might remember the wrongs that plagued you the day before. As you think back to twenty-four hours ago, you might forget about a problem. You need to stay motivated and confident.

As we proceed in our daily routines, we sometimes return to the mind-set we had before bed. Do not listen to music or loud noises when you first wake up. Instead of immediately sitting up, take five minutes to think about everything you plan to do during the day and any problems you might have. Whatever is happening is not as big a deal as you made it out to be. You can calmly focus on bad news because your body hasn't woken up yet. Go over everything you need to know about the situation. As you return to the issue during the day, focus on the best parts instead of the problems.

PATTERNS

Some people do the same shit over and over. Like video game characters, they only have a certain number of moves they can make. You can easily read someone's moves. The first is body language, which we all have subconsciously or consciously. It's the way the body is when we speak, move, think, attack, or defend.

Humans tend to describe how they feel in clusters. It is easy to read a person if you look at the cluster of behavior versus one single action. The same goes for traveling, eating, or recreational activities. Even if a person were to change his or her habits, it takes practice and training to change their patterns. A thrill seeker is still a thrill seeker in a shark tank or skydiving. Their activities and behaviors match their personalities.

Knowing yourself is important because people can tell your next move, including where you are going, when you don't. When you are still, they can no longer track you. You have nothing for them to feed off of. Anything you say or do is data for the next person to use.

No matter what message you are trying to convey, it's always going to say something. In poker, these actions or response are called tells. Tells are signals of emotion expressed in physical mannerisms. If you get a winning lottery ticket, your reaction might be a scream. If you are playing poker and have a winning pair you might act calm. To keep your tells to minimum, watch how people respond in different situations.

PASSION

Passion is being eager and enthusiastic about something you love. It can be a person, a place, or an idea that gives you meaning. It drives you to get something done every day. It contributes to your accomplishment.

Some people quit their jobs to become more successful in things they love. Passion helps when you don't make money the first year or two. Instead of trying to be a miserable bodybuilder, you might look forward to cutting the grass after leaving the gym. Maybe you enjoy cutting the neighbor's grass. That is something you go after. If you are in the game for money—and you get enough neighbors to trust you—you can profit. Get enough yards, and you can draw out a plan to make some real business decisions.

Self-respect is the basis of becoming a better person. Do what you love. Do what makes you look forward to getting out of bed. It might not be something you are proud to display in front of people, but it makes you proud to be alive.

PAY THE PRICE AND SHARE THE CREDIT

When you accomplish something with your team, share the rewards with them. You will reap the rewards with those who are close to you. Ungrateful people want to share in the rewards before you grant them permission. Anybody who cares for you will wait for permission before declaring they've won.

When you triumph over something, someone shouts, "We did it!" If they know it is not true, they might be seeking glory from your hard work. If the same situation occurs, and your loyal companions wait until you share in the harvest, they are. Anybody who does not acknowledge you for earning things in the first place should be watched closely. If your team saves the day, be sure to acknowledge them with praise and appreciation. Don't let anyone steal your thunder, but give them praise when praise is due. Do not shed light on your sacrifices. Instead, proceed as if they took nothing to achieve. Your team should never see you sweat or be burdened by a decision.

They should only see you use strength and character. Never give yourself away—and always share the spoils of your hard work.

PEOPLE MIGHT ATTACK YOU

When someone attacks you, it's usually for something you are good at. It doesn't matter what it is, they'll throw some shit at you in a heartbeat. You can be a great swimmer, but they will say, "You stay underwater too long, and your lungs will get messed up." You can be an excellent driver who knows how to drift around corners, but they will say, "That's not how you drive a car. You're going to jam the brakes." If somebody says something negative, it's probably what they want to see happen.

Pay close attention to what people are paying attention to. The details are going to be used to calibrate and adjust your weaknesses. Learn how to hold your breath for twice as long—or make sure those brakes are perfectly balanced. Do whatever you have to do to fix things before they become a concern.

Anybody can point out something they think is wrong with you. It is your job to take in their thoughts, appreciate the feedback, and prepare for what could do you harm in the future. Don't take their advice personally. Look at it as an imperfection they are trying to correct in you.

Most people are not willing to go after their dreams, but they will follow someone who is. Respect everyone's opinion of you, seek the truth, and imagine yourself as a piece of clay. Every time someone speaks to you about what they think is going to happen, they are trying to remove any bumps and make the clay a perfect sphere with no flaws.

PEOPLE DON'T CARE HOW MUCH YOU KNOW

Never come off as a know-it-all. No matter how much information you have, if people think it's out of pride and arrogance, they will shy away from what you say. Instead, only offer the most important topics. You have to be gentle when giving information to people, especially those who are less intelligent than you are. That's the way it is when it comes to helping others. You don't want to overburden someone with something they probably don't want to know in the first place. Always consider how someone might feel and whether they are worth informing in the first place.

Knowledge is a weapon, and information in the wrong hands can be deadly. Watch yourself when conversing to others. If you were locked in a cage and couldn't get out, what precautions would you take? What information would you keep inside? When people find out you genuinely care about them, they will believe every word you say. This is a trick that con artists use. They act friendly and then spew nonsense as they retrieve vital information from you. Instead of being a manipulator, offer selective honesty to people who need to hear the truth. Be sensitive about it. Share only what you need to with those who need to hear it at the right time. Be specific, show gratitude toward the listener, and be gentle with their egos.

PEOPLE GIVE THEMSELVES AWAY

All you have to do is observe somebody, especially if you know them. The second they begin to perform out of their nature, something has occurred that wasn't supposed to happen. Maybe they thought something would never happen to them. What variables provoked such a move? Did they have practice outside your knowledge? Who did they practice with? What is that person's relationship to you? Would they do something to protect you without you knowing it? Would that person defend you from other people without telling you? You have to account for why people do what they do and then suddenly shift. Listen to their words, the context, the format, and the timing. Why would they say it?

A friend or foe will always say what they feel. The brain is a current, and the mouth is a filter. Look, listen, and pay attention to the details of a person's behavior. Look for any abrupt changes. You can feed someone bullshit to see if word travels. If you tell a person something, and the information circulates, there you have it.

PEOPLE KNOW WHAT THEY ARE DOING

The first time someone disrespects you is the last time they should be allowed to. Don't waste time with anyone who can't see the good in who you are and what you represent. Most people will come off as friends and pose as allies when they are really trying to figure out your next move. Don't trust anybody who shows you their true hand. Once somebody crosses that line, you should consider it a warning.

On that level, people have a good idea of how they feel about you. Don't get caught up in gossip or ignore the signs. Don't leave yourself vulnerable in areas it would be a struggle to recover from. Snakes and backstabbers will fall before you and wait until you turn your back to strike. Nobody is innocent in the realm of adulthood, and nobody is as foolish as the absentminded leader.

The closest people to you will be the first to betray you. They might act as if something is wrong with you if they get caught. Most successful people say that friends and family hurt you because they can't accept the fact that you have outgrown them. That shouldn't stop you from proceeding in the future.

No one is lost to such a point that they can't tell what they are doing. Be wise in your judgment. Be slow to hire and quick to fire. The betrayal of someone close to you can be a warning of impending doom. The sacrifice of your initial judgment is worth the investment in the preservation of your hopes and dreams. If a friend gets caught, he or she might reveal other people who have bad intentions for you. Your friend sets off the alarms as a sacrifice and to weed out intruders. Always pay attention to people who worry for your safety. Betrayal is betrayal, and loyalty is loyalty.

PEOPLE AFFECT YOUR GOALS

In life, people will offer two incentives: positive or negative. It is up to you to decipher what their actions mean. How they affect you once the score has been tallied up. Over a six-month time span, if you count the points somebody has accumulated with you, you can see if the person is worth being around. There is not a right or wrong way to look at mental markers, but it would be wise to remove any potential threats. This system is one way to observe a person's actions. Don't tell the person how you are measuring them. Everyone starts at zero and works their way in whatever direction they choose. Be sure to keep track of the results. Twelve months is the maximum you should allow people to be around you before you make a decision.

PEOPLE DON'T OWN YOU

If your superiors disagree with a decision you make and betray you, it is because they can't control you. During your journey, you are going to encounter dozens of people who claim they care for you— and they will do anything to convince you of such. In reality, they have motives. They might use you as a stepping-stone to gain what they want.

You might meet an agent that can get you a role in a movie. If you miss your audition, the agent might fire you and say you are bad for business. Why would he do that if he had no intention of helping you? What will he say if you ask for a do-over? If someone is trying to help you, they will go out of their way to accommodate you with no strings attached.

PERCEPTION

Perception is a way of regarding, understanding, or interpreting something. It is a mental impression. The information the mind receives about people changes on a daily basis. What someone is feeling right now or thinking about you might change completely by the next day. Most people only care about themselves. Whatever someone is thinking about you is what they want to continue thinking about you. It doesn't benefit you to try to change what someone is thinking about you, especially when you don't know them.

Continue building the reputation you want by avoiding your perception of what others perceive. Think only about the goals you have in mind and what is required to achieve them. Thinking about the way others see you is a waste of time. The best way to keep track of the way people see you is to record yourself. As you measure the variations of what you do and how you do it—or what you say and how you say it—you will begin to see the patterns that affect what someone else sees.

Keep in mind what you think about yourself and focus on that. The way people see you is the way they want to see you. Hang around with negative people is saying that their actions and words are true and permissible by your standards.

PERSEVERANCE

Perseverance is defined as steady persistence in a course of action, a purpose, or a state, especially in spite of difficulties, obstacle, or discouragement. You will face many pitfalls and trials on your journey. Enjoy the lessons—and learn from them. A lot of people succeed every day, but you don't see their hardships.

Success requires a daily commitment. It doesn't come overnight, and if it does, it can leave just as quickly. All it takes is one mistake to send you back to square one. The best person to depend on in times of trouble is yourself. A basketball player who has potential but doesn't succeed can only blame himself or herself and the team. The fans can't go on the court and start playing. It doesn't work that way.

If the situation gets rough, stick it out. Keep moving forward. The harder the battle, the greater the reward. Look for a challenge every day. It should force you do work harder. If it comes easily, you are not challenging yourself enough. Endurance is the best teacher, and if you make sure your teacher is satisfied, you will never have to worry that you put in enough effort.

If you love what you do, the pain and suffering during the building stages will contribute to the victory. If you don't love what you do, you won't love the hardship it will bring.

PERSONALITY

Personality is the traits, habits, and experience that culminate in the thoughts one produces. Someone's personality will tell you what they are capable of doing, their character flaws, their ambitions, and how they will treat you when times get rough. Be sure to pay attention to how someone looks at themselves in the mirror. Pay attention to how they love themselves and how others feel about them.

Everyone has at least one enemy, and the person with no enemies has no friends. That person should be regarded as untrustworthy and a liability. That person will cause nothing but pain with the lies they tell you and themselves. If you have no enemies and have no one to overcome or challenge you, how can you ever be something? You are like a snake stabbing everyone in the back—friend and foe alike.

Be frugal with those you trust and uncaring with those you dislike. Your enemies will act like friends when you reach a certain level because you have so much to offer. To unlock certain doors, they must get the keys first. Befriending you is the easiest way to do that, but it requires the most work. They must watch your every move. People you can trust have your back and trust you. How much easier would it be to defend your mountain if you could put your back against a friend? The environments people come from will let you know what they are capable of.

PERSUASION

Negotiation is the exchange of resources for mutual benefits. Persuasion is the act of convincing someone that your terms are more suitable. It involves changing a person's value toward resources. Depending on who you talk to, persuasion can be difficult or easy. Negotiation is fast, and persuasion is slow. Negotiation can be expensive, and persuasion is free.

There are at least six universal principles to persuasion: reciprocity, scarcity, authority, consistency, liking, and consensus. Reciprocity is the practice of exchanging things with others for mutual benefit, especially privileges granted by one country or organization to another. When using this, people are obliged to give back what they receive first. Mutual agreements, like favors and invitations, work through reciprocity.

To maximize the psychological effect of reciprocity, you must be the first to give a personalized or unexpected gift. The second principle is scarcity, which is defined as the state of being scarce or in short supply. The third principle is authority, which is defined as the right to act in a specified way, delegated from one person or organization to another. This occurs when people follow experts in making decisions.

The next principle, consistency, is defined as the achievement of a level of performance that does not vary greatly in quality over time. It starts with looking for and asking for commitments. Small commitments add up to larger ones. A small sticker in the window of a home can have a dramatic increase in the number of yard signs in a neighborhood. Voluntary acts and public commitments are used for this.

The next principle, liking, is defined as a feeling of regard or fondness. People prefer to say yes to people they like. We like people who are similar to us, who pay us compliments, and who cooperate with us toward mutual goals. To harness the power of liking, be sure to look for similarities and give genuine compliments before you get down to business.

The final principle, consensus, is defined as general agreement. People will look at the actions of others to determine their own actions. Those six principles of persuasion are scientifically proven to have a massive impact on the psychological results of others. If you implement them in your travels, situations will transform into opportunities. To be persuasive is to have influence and understand the environment and reach negotiating terms.

PETS

A lot of times, people need a little pressure to get them going. A little extra responsibility forces them to make the right choices. What could be better than a pet? You can take care of a pet and be there when it counts the most. The sacrifices needed for survival will kick in and cause you to think differently. Having to make sure your animals are fed and sheltered will cause you to look at your expenditures differently. Instead of purchasing that favorite handbag or a pair of shoes, you will see that spending money on such items is futile. Why buy an expensive item you can't afford when you can buy something just as nice at a cheaper price and maintain a good life with your animal? Ever since I brought my two puppies home, my goal was to make sure they never went hungry and always had shelter.

A pet is a good way to release tension when you can't voice it to people. You can focus on any pressure you feel while petting, feeding, walking, or playing with your animal. Talk to your animals about your day—and see how they react. Animals can't talk and don't care about your troubles—and you shouldn't either. That energy will travel to your pet and bounce back to you as peace.

How can you be under such pressure when being calm and feeding your animal is all you need to do for the day? Don't worry about homework, a big boxing match, or a paper that needs to be faxed. Being calm, relaxing with your pet, and looking toward the future will suffocate whatever is making you uneasy. When people have kids, they thrive and go further. The thought of a starving child is too much to bear.

The way to decide what kind of pet to get is to determine which one makes you struggle the right amount physically and mentally. Animals can help you keep love in your heart and remain humble when everyone else is poisonous. Make sure the pet you choose will get through to your heart. Many people get a goldfish, a dog, or a cat. You must balance your life because a big dog could eat you out of house and home. A big cat can become a danger to you. A big fish could be difficult to feed. Exotic pets are for the more secure people. Don't get anything that would disturb the environment too much. Certain plants can harm the forest. Be careful—and enjoy your new friend.

PIPELINES

When you start facing bullshit, look at where its coming from. See what trouble it brings. Everything you face comes from a certain direction. On a road, you can immediately change direction. A pipe is more direct, and a set course is traveled. You can't see what's coming until you get to the end of the pipe. If someone were to give you trouble, imagine mud or shit traveling down the pipe. Send your own shit back down the pipe. By reversing the situation, you can discover the true intentions of the person. If someone talks behind your back, the invisible nature of their words travels as if through a pipe. You discover the issue at the end of the situation. Instead of letting it get to you, send your own words back through the pipe. Pay attention to the details and gather the available data.

PLAY THE FENCE

When all hell breaks loose, you might have to stand back and let things play out. Play the fence. After being driven in so many directions for so long, it's time to remove yourself from the game of truth and wait. When someone comes to your aid, they will immediately handle the situation. They will drive out the negative influences you are facing. Since you are not on the field when things get rough, you can see who is winning and what the outcome will be. Some people need to have their asses knocked straight out of the ballpark. Since you are on the fence, you can see the home run and who is flying toward the fence. If you want to save that person, you can. If they are on their way out of the stadium, you could start cheering and hoping more negative influences are knocked out of the park. Playing the fence means standing aside and letting someone else go to bat for you. They might have an advantage you do not have when it comes to the bullshit people are trying to send past you. Let someone else go to the plate and knock that mess out the park.

PLAY DUMB

In the beginning, the things people say and do might seem like a good idea. The things that are presented might seem like something you want to do. On your journey to success, you will face people who think they know everything. Some of the closest people to you will give you information. They aren't trying to disrespect you, but they have a bit of knowledge to give you. Acknowledge them with courtesy and display the same mentality.

Pretending to be less smart than you really are is a good way to retrieve information from people, especially if you can withhold knowledge of what they are talking about. When people discover how much you know, they lose faith in their ability to help you. Nobody wants to feel like the dumbest person in the room. Playing this role takes time and patience. Your look, appearance, and ranking don't play major roles because the conversation is most important.

If you can, bring down the judgment of others and learn to listen. The information you can receive from others is limitless. Everything has a bottom, and information is carried in the depths of people's minds. Become the go-to person with a higher position than others and a lower ear.

PLEASURE

Everything involves pleasing someone to one extent or another: performing in a classroom, performing on television, performing on a stage, performing on a basketball court, performing on a football field, or performing in bed. Talking to people is a pleasure you should master. When calling you, someone should expect to be entertained, thrilled, and educated. Develop the habit of telling people what they want to hear when you speak to them. Don't deceive people. Soothe them and remain humble.

People should receive comfort when speaking to you. Be firm in your affirmations toward others—and do not waver in your words. Your point should come as an expectation and not a surprise. Your victims should want to hear your words, but they should be more interested in your ideas.

The best way to exchange energy is to focus on making contact with people. Think about touching them before you touch them. If you brush their shoulders, think of the moment right before you make contact—and then make contact. Your mind will become aware of the person's higher consciousness making contact with yours. When touching this person, your blood pressure will go up.

Think positive thoughts about yourself—no matter what. The sweet sound of your lovely voice will completely disarm your adversary.

POISONOUS DEALS

Poisonous deals come from people who want to sabotage two parties. If your attorney sets you up in a deal to steal from another company, he or she is killing two birds with one stone. The third party has ill will toward you and someone else. In moments like that, the third party wants to make them crash into each other. It can be a case of someone trying to steal your company and making deals in your name. Your business will be misused, and the person conducting the activity is engaging in criminal acts. You have to fix the business, and the other person could be facing charges.

Another aspect of a poisonous deal is being told that you should sign on the dotted line without full disclosure of what you are winning or losing. When you do business with people, do background checks, credit checks, and up-to-date profit-and-loss statements. Scams can appear legitimate. Salt looks like sugar at first glance, and it is only when you sample that you discover what lies beneath the surface.

Most companies are reflections of the owners. If you get an indication that the owner shouldn't be trusted, be wary of signing any documents. The documents lock you in, and your signature on those documents can destroy your business. Check the details and look at all the numbers. A good business leader doesn't need help from anyone and looks for collaborations, which are equal partnerships in business. Be smart about getting into bed with new people.

POISONOUS PEOPLE

Poisonous people have self-destructive tendencies. They can't even trust themselves. It is best to avoid these people at all costs. They are out to hurt you and everyone around them. These people cannot be left alone, and they can cause trouble, friction between you and others, and total destruction.

Poisonous people have bad intentions toward you and other people. Try leaving them in charge of other people. When they are in control of other people, they will object to every command. Good leaders will weed these people out swiftly. What is life like for these people when they are alone? They often shoot themselves in the feet. They will screw over their friends and teammates. After you've been stabbed in the back, the poisonous person will turn around and try to destroy others. They don't like themselves and are self-destructive. They don't mix well with anything or anyone. Beware of their existence—and avoid crossing paths with them.

POKER FACE

Why would you show off for anyone else? Keep a straight face about your victories and losses at all times. No one should ever be able to tell what you plan to do, especially if you are preparing for an assault on the enemy. Straight-faced is the way to be when dealing with people you do not trust. It's not weird if no one can read your facial expressions. Keep your face solid, keep your emotions in check, and control your mood, tempo, and pace. Never let anyone drag you down.

Look people in the face and keep your composure. Showing off lets people know they are better than you. Don't gloat about your victories. Never look back. Never wear what you went through as a mask. Smile and don't get too drunk or high. People will notice if you become a different person. You always want to appear the same way.

PRACTICE THE ART OF PATIENCE

You can't allow yourself to be overwhelmed by circumstances that are out of your control. You can't let a situation become a burden.

Sometimes a break is necessary. You can always go back to the issue later. One of the greatest achievements is learning how to wait. Most animals have patience because they know the risk of going after a target too early. Patience is a useful tool to have in your arsenal. It can work wonders when no one else can help you. At some point, you might take the wrong path. You will have to wait until you return to the beginning. It doesn't take much to learn patience. All you have to do is learn how to wait. The key is to plan for waiting. Don't focus on the length of time you have to wait. Plan your next move. Take into consideration any time lapses that might hinder you. It's not always what you see in front of you that can be a problem.

You've made it this far. Why push yourself? If you have to execute a bit of patience, it might be a good time to rest. Enjoy every moment. Don't be so quick in your movements that you fail to notice the warning signs. Don't be so slow that you fail to see opportunities. Learn to wait. That is the best weapon for the journey to success. Time is the greatest teacher, and when you possess patience, all sorts of information will be revealed to you.

PRIDE

Pride is the feeling, deep pleasure, or satisfaction derived from one's own achievements. The associated achievements, qualities, and possessions are widely admired. Throw that garbage out the window because you have nothing to be prideful for. There is no such thing as pride. There is only your will, your way, and the compromises you make.

Pride is one of the most poisonous emotions because it comes from a mind-set of superiority. You have no one to feel superior to unless you can fly or walk on water. Otherwise, let go of anything in your heart that tells you that you are better than someone else. You are a human being with feelings, wants, and needs—just like anyone else. Unless you keep it in check, your pride will always get in the way of what is best for you.

You are always on the hunt for more knowledge. You should never have the time to reconsider someone else's judgment when trying to better yourself. Pride is an illusion that will mislead you into contesting the thing that will change your life. Pride is afraid of a detour. Pride is afraid to eat dessert second. Pride is absentminded. It's no wonder wars have been started by people with so much to give. Pride tells them to keep going when common sense tells them to stop. Be smart, do better than those who came before you, and humble yourself with love and humility. Humbleness is the cousin of pride. It's always there to take over after pride has been defeated. Before that happens, let humbleness step in. Make sure everyone is happy the first time something comes up.

PROCESS OF ELIMINATION

The best way to figure out situations is to draw out the key components and remove whatever has been eliminated. Persons, places, and things will linger, but after a while, they will remove themselves from the equation. Eliminating certain portions of a scenario allows you to pay full attention to the importance of what is there. A few techniques will help you in your pursuit of truth and success. This technique allows you to see things you might have missed in your assessment. An advanced theory of perception would give you an opportunity to see ideas and theories through someone else's eyes or thoughts. Write down the details and dynamics of things you are concerned about and then eliminate whatever is no longer part of the details.

PRUDENT STUDENT

A prudent student knows exactly what to study. Some people quit their cushy jobs to start new businesses. They have discovered themselves and found what gives them joy and meaning—even if it comes with a significant pay cut. Most people are good at one thing, but they fool themselves into thinking they are good at something else.

Good students never stop learning. They never stop educating themselves in simple matters that come with the territory. They usually know how to do everything they hired others to do for them. It's be wise to be familiar with what is going on so you don't get bamboozled and tricked out of your money. When you know how to do a profession, you learn the psychology that goes into being good at something. Knowing the proper terminology shows you take the job seriously.

If you never stop learning, you will notice that you can't stop learning. Making your mind hunger for knowledge makes other people seem slower. They will seem obsolete when you know the whole game inside out—and they barely know how to explain the tasks you need to do. Someone who can't ride a bike knows nothing about changing gears or what makes a chain slip. Experts know how drafting can pull a bike up a hill.

PURPOSE

Purpose is the reason why something exists. It is why things happen in your life. Be mindful of what you're doing. When someone cheats on a spouse, the other person probably knew it was possible. They gave their spouse the benefit of the doubt. When a car breaks down, you knew at it was possible. When food tastes bad or the service is bad, you knew what you were getting into.

You can learn a lesson from your experience. When people wrong you, it didn't happen for a reason. That person would have done the same thing to anybody else. You were just the victim because you were not wise in what you were seeking. You have to be vigilant and mindful of what you do. There are two types of people: people who like you and people who don't. Be smart about who bring into your life. Some people are destined to be destroyed. This world is a testing ground, and what you do determines where you will end up.

PUSH AND PIVOT

A good skill to have is the ability to dance. All the greatest martial artists know how to dance. I don't mean they are flexible. The essence of martial arts is the ability to remain calm and dance your way out of a situation. Maybe kicking some ass is part of the routine, but the training teaches you how to balance and control your body and your emotions.

A bully has no route but forward. You move left, right, up, and down with no problems. You move forward and backward. When something doesn't go your way, look at it as a good thing. When you need to get something done, it will work out for you. It will cost time or money. The only time you should get emotional is during a celebration. It should not bother you when a bank account closes or a document isn't filed on time. A small issue needs resolving, but it's nothing serious. If a bank account closed with a lot of money in it, then it would be a problem. Even then, the bank would notify you and offer a solution.

Let go of the control you think you have and maneuver through the hardships like a martial artist in a crowd. A pivot is a way to turn something in your favor. Imagine leaning on the heel of your right foot, catching a baseball with your right hand, spinning to the right, and throwing the ball with your left hand.

The pivot is the center of it all. It is the focal point in which everything is connected. When you turn, the whole table turns.

When you lean, the whole table leans with you. Learn how to control this dynamic when something goes wrong. A ball on a balanced table is easy. If the table shakes, the ball will fall off the table. Placing a pivot under the table gives you the ability to make the table dance and spin. You can keep the ball from falling off the table. Use a pivot to spin a bad situation in your favor.

PUTTING ON A SHOW

Don't get caught up with anybody who doesn't have the same importance as you. It will lead you into a world of trouble. People do things to make other people pay attention to them. Someone you have a disagreement with is likely to agree with you when no one is around. If a friend, coworker, or ally were around, the situation would be different.

People tend to crave attention in any situation. It could be the worst of the worst, and they still want everyone around them to pay attention to them. When they can't generate it, they use others to gain the eyes and ears of others. Don't be that beacon. When you notice that someone is making a spectacle, get away from the scene immediately. Being somebody else's puppet won't help you win. When you take your presence away from people like that, it leaves them no choices. You can crush their egos by ignoring them. Nobody wants to be the center of a bad joke.

QUESTION THROUGH LIFE

You should have a question for every answer in life. Every time you get a piece of information, the rebuttal should be an in-depth question about what is next. Ask so many questions that people get sick of talking to you and dread seeing you.

Questions are like shovels digging unexplored terrain. The more you know, the less likely you are to make a misstep. It might seem annoying to always ask questions, but think of it as a safety mechanism. If you ask people the same question, you are guaranteed different answers. Even if you ask the same person the same question, you will get a different answer. Why take a chance on not knowing enough when you could learn everything there is to know about a subject? You can decide what you should apply. Asking questions is a way to explore without experiencing failure.

The only question you might experience is whether you should ask a question in the first place. "If I ask this question, will the outcome satisfy my quest for knowledge and experience?" Some people will try to discourage you because they do not want to answer your questions.

QUICKSAND

Be careful not to attack something you can do not damage. You will only hurt yourself and sink your chances of destroying the opposition. Pursuing threats leaves you vulnerable to attacks and susceptible to defeat. You're only hurting yourself when you attack without calculating the outcome.

Always take a timeout before you go after any threats. The situation will work out in your favor—or it won't. Look at the effects it has on your progress. If it causes you to stop paying attention to other people, they have loosened the fabrics of your efforts and caused them to become capable of allowing you to sink.

If you are able to attack someone but it hurts you, you still do not have control. You might be sinking. The best way to analyze the situation is to understand that you have a problem and then sit completely motionless. As long as you don't move, you might sink— but at a much slower rate. As you begin to slow down, calm yourself. Always forgive yourself. You only get one chance at life. Do be hard on yourself. Do not panic when you realize the situation is out of your control. It is useless to fight back at first, but there is always a way to save yourself.

RAINY DAYS

Some people take rainy days as a fault. Some people take them as a relief. Rainy days are rainy days. This doesn't mean the end of the world. Sometimes things happen that are out of everyone's control. Does that mean you stop and give up? No, it means you take the good with the bad. Not every day is going to be the best day, and not every day is going to be worst day. When times get tough, you should be happiest because that usually means your hard work is manifesting into a physical creation.

Rainfall relaxes most people, and the same philosophy should be applied to the troubles you face on a daily basis. When the days are easy and everything is peaceful, you should wonder if something isn't right. If you are hard at work on something you love, the satisfaction should be from how much you get done. Try listening to rainfall while thinking about a stressful or frustrating ordeal. It's easier to concentrate on a subject if your mind is focused on one issue.

Your inner voice is constantly talking. The rainfall will cloud the noise in your mind, and your thoughts will form around the important subject. It's a great way to practice meditating and concentrating. When it rains, it pours. Put on your raincoat and boots and go to work. The only time you should be comfortable is when you don't have time to sit down. Other than that, you remain uncomfortable by not being busy enough. Rain can cause you to be cold and sick or clean and joyful. Water is your friend, and it cleanses the dirt from your shoes. Water can also show you where you have holes in your structure.

READING

Reading is fundamental and important in your day-to-day living. When you read, your mind grows in power and size. Your brain has the ability to expand if it wants to. When you read, it is like going to the gym and working out. Your brain becomes stronger and more durable. Processing information causes the mind to expand and contract. Reading makes problems easier to figure out. Reading will help you figure out solutions in the long run.

Architects should read books on structures, engineering, foundations, and materials. Sunlight makes people work harder and be more productive. In sales and business, psychology is a secret weapon. Sex sells. If you open a sunglasses stand in front of a lingerie store, you are 60 percent more likely to make a sale than in front of a bookstore. The mind can be altered.

REALIZATION IS A FORM OF BEING TOO LATE

There are two places you never want to realize something: a hospital or a battlefield. Either the sickness has taken hold of so much that there is no cure—or you are struck by a damaging blow on the battlefield. Either way, there is no saving you. You want to be as emotionally, mentally, physically, and spirituality fit as possible. Put yourself in a position to be aware of any upcoming challenges. Otherwise, you can be blindsided and suffer. The warning signs are always there. All you have to do is pay attention. The situation will always give you answers and the physical necessities to fix them. If you have a flat tire, you need to stop and put air in the tire. If you pay attention to the tires, you will see the problems earlier. Pay attention to the struggles and what they force you to do. That is the answer during times of stress and frustration. Do not be naïve to the problems you believe are gone and can't come back. If you fail to destroy a problem in the beginning, it will come back tenfold. Be wise in the way you handle uncontrollable scenarios and have faith in your ability to correct puzzling shifts in plans.

REEL THE REINS

Don't give anyone the opportunity to take control of your life. When you reel in the reigns, you stop moving forward in a way that is not conducive to your life. Stop giving people a way to harm you. If you stop trying to control a sled with reindeer, they will stop, get tired, or lose direction, which slows down their momentum.

You will be tested by someone close to you. Whether you are ready or not is up to you and how you handle the situation. What you put in is what you get out. If you don't want trouble from anybody, don't give it to anybody. Sometimes acting as if nothing happened is the best way to move forward. After a while, a person or group will decide to cause trouble. Times will get tough, and you will need to get off the sled. There will be traps. You are on the right course, but the route needs to be adjusted to serve you better.

REASONING

Never let someone know when you've discovered something new about them. Ignore the moment you figure out a solution to a problem. Just execute. There is no point in trying to communicate with people you can't communicate with. It wastes your time and energy on a situation you probably didn't create.

Your enemies or adversaries may be willing to listen. Never pride yourself on the understanding of people you do not trust. It's like trying to shout over a speaker system. Why waste your time when whatever is causing trouble for you is there to create a problem in the first place? You should always be able to understand yourself and be reasoned with. If a situation is provoking you to lose control, don't let it.

You understand every aspect of the dilemma you are facing. You can accomplish much more if you have the ability to think at all times. Don't be so angry that there is no turning back. Some people love attention and want someone to be on them all the time. Don't be confused when people try to explain their problems to you.

RECOGNITION

We all crave recognition in our lives. The most dangerous temptation is taking credit for another person's accomplishments. Recognition is probably one of your worst enemies on your way to the top because people become jealous and envious. If they can take you out, they think they can have what you built.

A lot of people sit around and wish they were someone else. Your trophies, luxuries, accomplishments, and glory are all up for grabs at all times. Be careful who you trust and break bread with. Don't share the spotlight. Everyone craves attention, and social media makes it worse. Save your important positions for your most dedicated workers. Praise and raise those who deserve your well wishes. Make sure that anyone who joins your team understands that what you are trying to achieve is more important than money or fame. The lifestyle and good deeds you live by are the most important things. Protect yourself and those around you from the blood-sucking leeches.

REFUSE HATRED

Hatred is the most important topic you will face. Even on a clean road, you will need to eliminate anger from your well-being or become something you do not want to be. You have to be positive at all times. Shit is going to rock your boat constantly during your journey, but that doesn't mean it has to stick with you for life.

Admit that things hurt, and let go of the other bullshit. Dust yourself off, keep going, stay true to yourself, and be happy. Don't follow the urge to beat somebody's ass, punch someone in the face, or say something hurtful. Don't take that road. Do not sabotage other people's lives. Stay authentic. Don't let your attitude poison your mind. Don't hate people.

Love the pain and pleasure and feel the joy of victory overcoming everything you face. Deny yourself all the things you want to do gain retribution. Take the high ground with the long road. In combat, gaining higher ground provides better shots at the enemy. Don't let someone's hatred for you make you do something you wouldn't normally do.

REHEARSAL AND ROUTINE

As progression toward the top becomes easier, you begin making plans, conducting research, and initiating experiments. Your personal life will become a routine. Direct your attention and focus on what is important. You might save time by wearing the same outfit every day. That routine will save you time.

Planning your outfit saves time. Routines save time. Rehearse what to say at social events. Confidence helps with executing anything you want, and rehearsals are the foundation for confidence. Small routines can help you move forward faster. Rehearse whenever and wherever possible to get a task done with precision, accuracy, and finesse.

REGRET AND GUILT

Someone who regrets something is liable to do something to remove it. They will continuously come at you with the same bullshit that started everything in the first place. This includes family and friends who might have done something wrong by accident. If they continue to do something you dislike or won't apologize, that should be a good indication of where you stand with that person. It doesn't matter how beautiful you thought the person was—let them go immediately. People who genuinely care about you do not want to hurt your feelings.

If you have regrets in your system, evaluate what is going on and accept whatever things you can't change. That might mean taking the blame for something you did not do. Screw it. It's not like it's going to kill you. Be careful about your emotions. Don't let people affect how you feel. No one is perfect, and putting people above you will only lead to disappointment. The best way to limit regret is to never do anything you don't agree with. If the guilt eats the person up inside, they might attack you.

REMEDIES

A remedy is a medicine for a disease or injury. A medicine is a chemical, an herb, or a combination that provides a solution to a problem. The difference between a remedy and a medicine is the way they are created. While medicines have the purpose of fixing a problem, remedies are solutions that fix the problem in a specific way for a particular situation.

If your dog has a skin problem, you can go to the veterinarian for medicine. A much cheaper remedy can be found at home and is probably more effective because it is natural. A little soap and some baking soda will solve the problem for most dogs. The solution might stop that pesky skin problem from spreading. A remedy will save time and effort.

You can do the same thing if you pay close attention. A remedy for going to work would be getting a bike instead of a car. A car is the medicine, and a remedy is the bike. In school, the medicine is to not fight and avoid a certain person. A remedy is to get someone else to fight them. A remedy fixes problems via natural causes. It uses cause and effect to create a situation of relaxation and trust and lets nature take its course. There is more than one way to fix a problem.

RESILIENCE

Resilience is the capacity to quickly recover from difficulties. A little bit of thick skin goes a long way. You are going to be tested until you break or don't break. When the going gets tough, take your ass to your room and cry if you need to. Never fade, never tire, and continue to pursue whatever you seek.

A good way to tell if you are on the right course is if bad things happen to you. You might get in trouble, or people might not like you.

Be reasonable in your ambitions—but know that things will get bad. Don't think everything is peachy and perfect. Expect some pain and scars along the way. The best way to keep from experiencing painful situations is to keep what you do a secret. Don't be afraid to hurt alone. The more you speak, the more trials and tribulations you will face. You don't have to. Extra trouble comes from talking too much and letting people know what the deal is with you. If no one can figure out your next move, they won't know where to find you. All they can do is wait for you to reveal what you have done. Be strong, look in the mirror, and love what you see.

If someone hurt you once, they will probably do it again. If someone thinks and behaves like the last person, you know what to expect and what to avoid. Pay attention. You have to go through some suffering. When you suffer, keep smiling and be happy. Smile at yourself. Find a mirror and smile when things go well or things go badly.

RESPECT

Respect is a feeling of deep admiration for someone or something elicited by their abilities, qualities, and achievements. We all know someone we feel these things for. Some people are like superheroes to us. We feel these things because they do things or have done things that you wish you could do. You might be a little intimidated, and that's fine. That makes individuals respected, interesting, and beloved. Maybe they have nothing to lose. Maybe they have an advantage.

Respect is earned and not given. It takes a lifetime to build and a second to lose. Be careful in how you treat people. Always look out for the small guy. Be wise about who you call a friend. Be smart in how you approach people. Be good to yourself. Association can do the most damage. You can be the best person to be around and celebrate events with—and then be found with a wicked person who no one cares for. How will people look at you? Eagles fly with eagles, and snakes slither with snakes. Birds of a feather flock together. Take that to heart.

The moment you notice yourself being introduced to someone who you do not approve of, be cautious. Examine those who bring these types of people around. Have pride in what you avoid. Association will do the most damage. When your life is under control, you attract much more than what you like and dislike. Your ambitions are real, and what you seek has a mind of its own. A planted tree attracts bees, bears, and axes. That might not be what you set out to do, but it's the end result. With others, be mindful of how you speak. Carry yourself as if a camera was always placed on your shoulder. Everyone is always watching. That type of mind-set will allow you to be careful in your deeds, actions, and words.

RESPOND MORE AND REACT LESS

Never let your temper get the best of you. There are plenty of things that might make you lose control of your emotions. Some things will be fixable. Some things will not be fixable. A way to determine all the factors is to pay attention to what happens. Instead of making snap decisions, check out the problem and see if you can take care of it by moving slower.

When something you don't like happens, don't do anything until the next day. Give yourself time to go through your subconscious and understand every perspective and angle. People will stop approaching you with their troubles because they understand your focus will be directed. This could be good or bad. If bringing something to your attention means definite destruction, it doesn't matter how long it takes to happen.

You should always be calm when responding. No one should ever know how you feel about something when you are responding. The less people know, the better. Calculate all the variables before coming up with a solution. Relax, stay calm, and focus on the root of something you don't like.

Like a robot, determine what's important. Crunch the numbers, destroy or execute the solution, and resolve the issue. You are making all the decisions. Give yourself enough time and access. You could be wrong—or something could be missing from your knowledge. Don't lose your temper, act loud, or make a scene.

You put yourself at risk when you react to something because you don't know what areas might be affected. You can hurt yourself if you lash out to stop something. Figure out a way to stop problems from functioning properly. Survey how the engine works, toss a big wrench in the engine, and mess everything up.

REVERSALS

There is a silver lining to every situation. All you have to do is look for it. You always have a chance to reverse a situation, but it might take a little more time. The key is to not let it slip away. The key to not letting it slip away is to focus on why the situation exists and how it can be resolved or dissolved. Pay attention to how you face anything you're going through.

In reversals, you are turning bad into good. The point of a reversal is to adjust your attitude. Don't let anyone anger you over nothing. If it doesn't cause you harm, screw it. Why get bent out of shape for people and what they do? People are not dolls. Why get mad? Don't be a control freak. Instead of losing your temper, just watch.

Anybody who attacks you repeatedly is jealous of you and what you are capable of. They are trying to diminish your ambition and will to succeed. Watch how things change when you observe their attacks and gestures. Once you discover their weakness, lead each person involved down a path to reverse one good time. Pretend it's a basketball game. Wait for them to go to the rim and steal the ball at the last moment. Bring them down to the other end and slam it on them.

Don't be too quick to stop someone from making a fool of themselves. Let whoever is trying to put you in a bad situation put on a show and gather as many people as possible. You want to steal the show and take everyone who was watching. If people are stupid enough to believe what others say about you, use that to your advantage. Prove that the person saying bad things about you is a dumbass. They will turn and never believe them again.

RIGHT PEOPLE RESPOND THE RIGHT WAY

The best way to know how someone feels about you is to say nothing while casting stones in the water. The waves will continue for days, months, and years. That will force your associates to make a choice. Do they believe you are a threat or a safety net for others?

The people who have wronged you will always take something you do in defense offensively. They never liked you from the day they met you, and as you begin to heat up the situation, they begin to get uncomfortable. This discomfort will force your associates to grin and bear it or flee. It doesn't matter how you behave or treat people because the ones who love you will always favor you.

Take no offense to those who betray you or leave you. They were never your friends to begin with. Those people had their own agendas, and when you no longer fit, it is time to get away from you. The right people will automatically get the message and know exactly what to do. If your secret message is to flood the room, they will know exactly where to run and where to hide until you are finished.

Don't let people fool you with a few nice deeds. Everyone knows what the deal is with you. You have to relay the message and watch the responses and reactions of others. Be passionate in your dreams. Do whatever you need to protect them. They will protect you while you slumber. Those who love you will smile in the face of your actions because they trust you and know who you are.

RITUALS

This should be a routine that makes you feel great. This activity should take you away from friends and family and be geared toward doing something for someone who was there for you in the beginning.

A ritual is an activity done for a religious purpose, but you can also conduct an activity or a ceremony for someone you lost.

You don't necessarily have to be religious to do a ritual, but the activity does include a ceremony to represent a faith. Someone has played a majestic role in your life if you have any dreams of success. Being successful sometimes involves walking by faith and not by sight. Someone in your life was always telling you that you would make it. These people are the spiritual anchors you need to pay homage to. If it weren't for them, you probably would have talk yourself out of moving forward.

Always bring flowers and a smile when visiting a gravesite, stopping by a hospital, or making a house visit. Do not let the memory of those who had your back in the beginning go unappreciated. Those are the people you should always look out for—no matter what happens. When you get to the top, they will not be surprised at all. They will continue to support you. Even with your new bells and whistles, your day ones will still use your childhood name and welcome you with open arms. In a way, this is negating what you have accomplished. At the same time, the message is that you're the same person to them. It's humbling having a ritual to keep your mind level.

SACRIFICE

Sacrifice means giving up on something you want to keep, especially to get or do something else or help someone. You better be ready to throw it all down if you have to. Be ready to delete and add up everything you need to move people out the way. There is no way you're going to be able to gain access to success without losing people, spending money, and becoming enemies with those you never thought possible. It's inevitable. No one you thought was coming with you will be there at the finish line. There will be no friends drinking sacred elixirs of youth on your own private island. There will be no spaceships. You will not be the richest people.

You need to wake up and smell the fresh air. No one is coming with you, and if they do, they better be willing to work. Those who join you are going with you on your terms. Anyone who joins you has to join on your terms—nothing more and nothing less. Plenty of people will want to join or buy themselves in, but they must be willing to put in the time, effort, blood, sweat, and tears you are willing to sacrifice. Be ready and able to leave the life you have at a moment's notice to gain access to that which is most important to you.

What you create is a part of you, and you need to be aware that your baby needs love and nourishment. Any mother in the animal kingdom would kick ass for her babies. The father is even worse when he's around, but that is Mother Nature. In human standards, either parent would annihilate you for coming near their children. The same goes for a work of art you've brought into the world. It doesn't have to be alive, but it comes from your existence and well-being. Protect what's yours. If you want to succeed, success should be the air you breathe, the food you eat, the sleep you need, and the water you drink. If death is the most absolute way to keep your ambitions intact, be ready to pass on the message to another. Be ready to give flesh and blood if necessary to keep your venture going.

SAME WAY IN, SAME WAY OUT

The course of action that got you into trouble will also get you out of trouble. The same course of action for success will lead to more success. Don't be mistaken by the thoughts and actions it took to put you wherever you are now. Use positive thoughts and actions to move toward success.

Every step you took led to the results you are experiencing. Sometimes small decisions can mean life or death. A woman picked up a coin before crossing a major intersection. As a result, the car that was on a course to hit her never triggered the tragedy that almost happened that day. Looking at the ground and picking up the coin changed her fate forever. You need to examine your decisions. That coin created a close call, but that isn't always going to be the case. You might have to retrace your steps, backtrack, or start from the beginning to stop trouble from going further or cease the destruction a foe might have created for you.

SCRATCH A LIE—FIND A THIEF

People lie all the time. A small lie or a big lie—a lie is a lie. Some lies are efforts to protect you from a greater danger than you can handle. Some lies are given to stop from gaining more knowledge of a situation. Some lies are given to obligate you to make a choice you wouldn't normally make. You have to look at the people who have to lie and the purpose in the lie. When somebody has to lie, they no longer have control of a situation.

If someone has to lie, more than likely it's because they are trying to alter the course of a money stream. Anytime someone tells a lie, you should always take note. Nobody should ever have to lie to you, and when they do, it should be insignificant. You will be lied to, and you will have to lie, but that doesn't mean you can do it without good intentions. When you discover that you have been lied to, don't let the person know you are aware of it. Instead, observe what they have lied about. What do they want you to know or do? It is like theft. Don't be naïve with those who give you false information or mislead you.

SECOND TO NONE

Always go for the second-in-command if you are trying to convince someone you should be part of their team. It's the best way to prove yourself. If their friends or associates see you, it works out better for you. Who better to say good things about you than the person your target has to see every day?

In addition to gaining the approval of the second-in-command, you demonstrate your ability to lead and follow. Those who come later will likely understand that you mean well and are trying to keep the ship afloat. Those ahead can trust that you bring great qualities to the team. If everyone moves as one unit, you are bringing the pieces closer. When seducing anyone's second-in-command, understand that this person is the best friend and knows the ins and outs of the entire group. Going up the chain of command provides a great argument when it's time to bring you aboard. That person should be your friend. The second-in-command is the manager and a reflection of whatever you want to be a part of. This technique works with men or women and socially or seriously. You are not trying to take over anyone's life by convincing their second-in-command to like you. You are learning the ins and outs of the group and shaping yourself into the right-sized puzzle piece.

SEEK FIRST TO UNDERSTAND

It's unlikely that people will understand you when you want them to. Most likely, your message will always be interpreted the wrong way. Inevitably, most people who hear your message will be offended. If this is ever the case, does it mean you should never speak again? Does it mean that those who don't understand you are the enemy? No. It means that some people will take you more seriously than others do. If you mean well and relay positive energy in your message and efforts, they should not be offended or angry. That person could take what you say to heart and need a little more time to see your point of view.

Let go of what you believe in when you seek it in others. Work and move as if no one will ever see your way of thinking. To see someone's point of view and understand them, be stronger, more merciful, and more understanding than ever. Perception is the ability to see yourself through other people's eyes. That is the key to understanding someone who might not be aware of your way of thinking.

Stop trying to convey any kind of message and lead people anywhere they do not want to go the first time you tell them to. It is not worth the time or effort to worry about one or two people when thousands will love you the first time you appear. Take your time with those who believe in you. Forgive those who might not understand or like you. Leave them behind and focus on those who need you immediately. If you are capable, make your way back to win over those who might find you interesting. If not, keep moving.

SELLING WOLF TICKETS

People who talk too much are selling wolf tickets. They are selling interest in an area they are not willing to go. Other people sell their knowledge to personal groups and events. Some people make threats or boast about talents they might not have.

When it comes to purchasing your way into societies, products, and private or public events, you should spend as much as possible. Your interest in others should be so high that when somebody introduces a friend, the friend should already be familiar with you. That is a secret weapon because it says you are more than just a customer who is seeking knowledge. It says you are a student who is seeking wisdom and trust in your field. This ability is impressive because it reveals a sense of trust between you and others.

If more than one friend is familiar with you, that means you are willing to pay. It means you are worthy of respect. As your presence increases, their concerns will become geared toward who you know and who you would like to meet. Your reputation will create an aura that you are a serious, well-known person who seeks those who are worthy of your time. The money and effort you invest show that you are willing buy a ticket to the show.

SHAPE-SHIFTING

You should be able to take on the form of anybody to get a job done. It doesn't matter how they look or sound—you should always know how someone would react or think in a situation and become that person. They will try to use this technique on you, which is why it is important to know everything about everybody around you.

At a moment's notice, you should be able to take on the role of everyone around you. A little skill in being someone else is important. Spies are effective because they know how to watch and listen to those they need to be like. In the movies and comics, a shape-shifter assumes the role of someone else perfectly. As a shape-shifter, you can become present in the ranks of your organization. If you know everyone around you and understand relationships, it should not be a problem to find the wrong people around you.

SHIT ROLLS DOWNHILL

Never get caught on the bottom of any list for too long. The troubles and problems people release for others to do will fall upon you if you're not careful. Any unwanted task or annoying point will fall upon you. There is always someone in charge and someone who follows. You don't have to be one of these people, but you will want to be toward the top.

Realize the importance of having a structure, respect the position you started out with, and move toward the top of the food chain as soon as possible. Arrive early, stay late, impress the boss, complete all jobs, and excel to the top of the pyramid. Achievements take time and patience. It is important to keep moving.

Look at the lowest in rank and see if he or she finds the job worth having. Watch how the ranking members fight over doing tasks to rise in rank and position. A healthy fight is proper, but deception and sabotage are indicators that rising in the ranks is infrequent. Be wise in who you choose to follow. Be smart in how you begin and finish a job.

If a big enough load of shit comes down, get out of the way—and let it roll down the food chain.

SOCIETIES

People build and create who they want to succeed. You will never be successful without the support of others. Your enemies will try to use influence to make someone else seem better than you. They will make a thief or a person who you don't like appear to be more dominant than you. The scoundrels will say your enemies' support was fair.

It is like working hard to get into professional sports—and then having somebody you don't like weasel his way into your spot. The agents and coaches pretend that he earned it on his own. A way to defeat this situation is to apply yourself. The way to start is to separate yourself from the falsehood that tries to claim you.

People who lie, cheat, and try to take your name will try to suppress your skills and get ahead. They will feed off of you until there is nothing left. They will eat away at your existence. As a skillful thinker, you will find the weak points of your enemy to gain the upper hand. Don't worry about people who don't support you—or even those who do. You have to worry about your enemies' intentions and plans.

You can march around all day in sports until it's time to put up some points. You keep building status, continue to train, and develop an arsenal for later use. Eventually, you will get the opportunity to show the right people what you are capable of. After making all this noise, someone at the top of the food chain will be waiting. That is when you present your skills and let the copycat gain all the attention of the crowd. It's time to put up or shut up. You will always have the chance to prove once for all who the owner and creator of something special is—even if it's not your ability that will score. It could be a project you spent your life trying to make a reality. Be persistent and resilient.

SOLITUDE

The state of being alone is a skill you better master if you want to survive. There are two types of people in this world: the people who can sit in a room alone with no interaction and those who can't. The people who can't are the most powerful people because being on top means being alone. It's lonely at the top, and there are never four or five leaders in an organization. It is just the leader, their organization, and the foundation. If you enjoy being by yourself more than being around people, you will never have to worry about making friends. Being alone requires being comfortable with spending time by yourself.

The loneliest people cannot relate to or understand each other. Why would you want to go through something like that? Why would you want to be around people who only like you for your appearance? You might only meet two or three people in your life who genuinely like you for you. The rest will be there for the way you look.

Practice sitting in a room with nothing besides a chair. Learn how to think in quiet places without any distractions. Eventually, your mind will reprogram itself to enjoy being alone. There is no such thing as loneliness when you have the ability to think for yourself. People who object to you wanting to be alone do not possess the ability to think for themselves. You should be able to sit in a room with someone and be completely silent. You don't have to converse with people all the time to communicate. Being alone allows you to focus on whatever comes out of your mouth.

SOMETIMES LESS IS MORE

At some point, doing things for others—entertaining people, achieving your goals, and making physical gestures—will reach a limit. When this limit is reached, a new plateau will be reached. Everything has a limit, a threshold, and when these barriers are breached, less is more. When you go deep enough in water, the pressure will cause pain. Enough pressure will cause you to stop going fast or deep.

If you hit someone enough times, a bruise will form. This is a sign that the body has reached its limit of endurance. If you fill a piggy bank with enough money, you will not be able to fill it anymore. You have reached its limit. The limits and barriers in these scenarios might not make much of a difference in your life.

The value in what you do should increase with the amount of effort you contribute. If the value of what you are doing doesn't increase your stature, rank, finances, or wisdom, you are doing something wrong. A professional is defined by how many times they do something and by the expertise they can offer. How many surgeries does a doctor conduct before becoming a master? A surgeon's skill set, expertise, and experience separate them from the rest. They could have done surgery on many elderly people, but what happens if a child needs to be saved? Set your mind to becoming a master in your field as soon as possible. Always seek to be valued and experienced in everything you do. A one-punch knockout comes from repetition, accuracy, and experience.

SPACE

A vast vacuum surrounds our world. Space controls everything around you. Have you ever noticed the control you have when you move away from people? Separation gives you control. Space is the greatest teacher. You can empower yourself with space. You have the ability to isolate your mind from any concerns that might plague you.

In separation, you will notice details and facts you never knew existed. A point will come when you will not answer the phone, open the door, respond to an email, post on social media, or leave your inner sanctum. You will figure out the advantage of being by yourself. That doesn't make you strange or bad. It makes you strong and wise. The most powerful people are not afraid of being alone. Many people claim to have all these friends who don't really exist. People choose to follow, and that changes daily. You have all the power if you have the ability to separate yourself from things you dislike. People will always try to gain the upper hand. Keep the distance between you and everyone you know at a minimum. Set a certain length—whether by phone call, fax, email, or visits—and leave it that way. Never allow anyone to dictate the distance you have from anything you care about. If you want to see someone in certain ways, keep it that way. Always be in control of your space.

SPEED

Speed has no relevance for those who know where they are going. The tale of the tortoise and the hare was a revelation for people who believe all is lost—and there is no hope. It doesn't matter how long it takes you to get somewhere. If you are meant to be there, the path will open for you.

People can outmaneuver you, outpace you, or even outthink you. If where you are going has a valid purpose to who you are, it doesn't matter. Someone seems faster because of what was predicted. If you know where someone is going to be before they get there, you can take a shorter route to meet them there. All you have to do is figure out where they are trying to go and see the bigger picture.

A thief only has one goal: to take something from you. You have to discover why, how, and where it will serve them. It takes time, but you must learn who and where your enemies are and the purposes of their actions. You must learn the end result. You appear faster than someone else, but you just know where they're going to be before they get there. Never be intimidated by someone who appears to be faster than you or who has an easier time doing something it took you ages to do. They cheated the system and bent the rules. It will not benefit them in the long run. Everyone gets out what they put in. A rush job usually has a few loose screws. A speedster usually runs out of gas.

STACKING

When completing a goal, task, or chore, scheduling, or building a structure, you want to set the regiment up to stack that chews itself up. When one job is done, the stack drops down like building blocks. You want the job to be done before doing the next job. The stack you create begins to drop down—with or without your permission. To keep up the pace, you have to continue to work and stay on point. You can set anything up like that. In doing so, you create a schedule that doesn't alter the goal you are trying to achieve.

The occurrences may be out of your control, which will leave a gap in the stack. The order remains in your control. If you leave the stack alone, you can pick things up again later. You can picture the blocks like a tank wheel. The giant chain goes around as you move forward and tumble into one another. They crush any obstacles in the way, and if you stop, the tank will stop. Keep moving forward— and don't let things get in the way of your progress.

STAND ON THE SHOULDERS OF GIANTS

Don't try to reinvent the wheel. Take an idea—and make it better! If you see someone doing better than you, emulate what they are doing and add your spin to it. It's not copying if you offer your expertise for a price to someone who might lack your talents. The price will sustain your way of living and give you the freedom and time to focus on thinking outside the box and creating more ideas. Extra help is people offering help for concepts and creations you might not be aware of. Everybody doesn't know everything, and you can make a living for yourself by helping people ride their waves. This technique will help others achieve their dreams. When you can't develop more ideas, you can't seem to get it up. When you don't know how to make more beautiful pieces of art, join those who have not made it to that plateau. This might require going back to the bottom of society. That is completely okay.

Creating innovation is not an easy task. Helping others and bringing more people aboard your vessel is important when building structure. Standing on others' shoulders and allowing people to stand on your shoulders is not disrespectful to you. It's a pat on the back. It is protection to stand with a giant when you don't know what to do. It's only dangerous when you become complacent in your ambitions. If the money, ideas, influence, and creations stop flowing within you, take a break to soar in the skies and ride on the shoulders of the people who broke the barrier of cluelessness.

STIMULATION

Stimulation is arousing interest, enthusiasm, or excitement. If you can't do it, get out the kitchen. People should enjoy every minute of being around you. They should enjoy being in your company, speaking with you, and doing other things. The time spent in your company should be thoughtful, pleasurable, and educational.

Don't waste time with those who do not take an interest in being around you. If they enjoy being in your company, they will enjoy your jokes and other offerings of entertainment. It takes practice, but before you know it, you will be able to stimulate even the worst of the worst people.

You shouldn't subject yourself to people you don't like. It puts a strain on you as person and what it means to hang with you. Your inner character should always shine when you spend time with people and when you are alone. Anyone who is talking to you should enjoy you without even knowing what you look like. Work on being someone everyone enjoys without them looking at you or knowing what you look like. That is when you have mastered stimulating people.

Comedy is the easiest and most effective way to disarm someone when meeting them or entertaining a group. People prefer to be stimulated in various ways. You should definitely appeal to the senses of each person to make a personal connection.

STRATEGIST

Always keep a backup plan, a way out, and the ability to shift around your goals. If you can't do "A," shift to "Z." If you can't do one, shift to three. Have backups for whatever you need to get done. Don't focus on the small things—focus on the bigger picture. Mistakes and miscalculations will inevitably mess up your schedules and plans. That is okay. As long as the big picture stays in focus, you don't have to worry about much.

Plans are essential for the offense and defense. You need it whenever something goes right or wrong. In most situations, you need a map of all the activity you conduct on a daily basis. A map or drawing offers you a chance to view the details in the movements of people, places, and things. The best strategists know all the details of their companies, households, groups, and associations. They know all the threats that exist. You should be able to tell where everyone is. Do not forget to be evasive in revealing this information because people will keep track of you.

STICK TO YOUR GUNS

Whenever a decision is made—no matter how bad or good the outcome—you must stand your ground. Giving up is saying the other person is right, and you forfeit your chance to prove your point. Situations may be beyond anyone's control. Instead of losing your temper, getting upset, or losing sight of the victory from your accomplishments, think of what you are proposing as a test.

If you ever had to accuse someone or make a decision based on someone, you know you can be wrong sometimes. Anytime you are forced to make a decision that no one else agrees with, it doesn't mean you are wrong. Instead, it's a test to see how well you know yourself and anyone else around you. Even if you turn out to be wrong about whatever you are trying to prove, be proud of yourself for standing firm.

You have to be as firm as the ground you stand on to succeed. The foundation to anything has to be the strong, including the thoughts behind your actions. Don't be hard on yourself if you are wrong about something. Remain firm when it's all said and done.

STEPPING-STONES

Everything is a stepping stone—situations, acquaintances, scenarios, problems, and mishaps. The goal is to step over them. You must acknowledge what the problem is and then come up with a solution. Great mountains have been climbed and are in history books. It is the same for every situation in life. Those mountains are nothing more than bumps in the road for some. Climbing a twenty-thousand-foot mountain is spectacular, but once it's done, it's time to move on.

To step is to walk forward, and to walk forward is to be in motion. To be in motion is to have a destination. To have a destination is to have somewhere to be. To have somewhere to be is to have a goal or objective. To have a goal or objective is to have a purpose. To have purpose is to know what you want out of life and go after it without anyone or anything stopping you.

A stepping-stone tried to trip you up, but you stepped over it and continued on your path. Many things will get in your way and go in your favor on the way to the top. Learn the difference between something that is easily stepped over and something that you have to go around. Either way, there is nothing you can't overcome with a little time and patience.

STEPS TO A START

There are five main steps on the course toward success: research, enrollment, trial, progress, and graduation. Each step will be a challenge that will require a different level of intelligence. Research is what you look up and identify as something you want to be a part of. During your research, you should always look toward something you enjoy. It doesn't matter if it's profitable as long you have a passion for it. In the end, it will become profitable. Your interest will grow into something that can help others.

Enrollment is the process of becoming part of a learning facility, program, fraternity, or group that will teach and guide you to the level of perfection you need to become recognized in your field. Trial is going through the motions, burdens, obstacles, and foes who to throw you off course. Get through it. Keep going for the sake of those who depend on you for leadership.

Progress is coming to an end in your field of expertise. You are almost at the end of the road, and the path you took is starting to get brighter for you. Focus on succeeding. Even if you are the only one left from the beginning, leave the others behind if you have to. Graduation should be considered an achievement. Take little pride in the ceremony because the real test is what you do afterward. That is when it's time to demonstrate your skills. Don't oversimplify the tasks you will be faced with, and don't overthink what it takes to get the job done.

STOP SIGNS

This is a bit different than following your gut instinct because it comes from something you're physically doing that isn't working in the way you thought it would. If you start a business and your sales aren't progressing in a timely fashion, you could be doing something wrong. If no one is interested your product—and you are making no sales—it's time to rethink your business strategy. If nothing is working after a certain time, stop! It's that simple.

A stop sign is put in place for you and somebody else on the other end of the road. You can ignore the stop sign if you want to, but your next steps are at your own peril. Appreciate a stop sign when you face one. You have been told to stop. Take a temporary break. The victory or loss will be important in your growth.

STRESS

Stress is mental or emotional strain or tension resulting from adverse or demanding circumstances. It is everywhere we turn. With healthy stress, there is not too much pressure on you. You can take a break and come back to finish. The stress of running an operation or managing a business is hard on the body and the mind. You have personnel to be concerned with and the objectives of the company. CEOs can suddenly take a leave or retire. It is not the success that is such a burden. It is the stress of managing and making sure things go according to plan.

In the mind-set of creating something, the wisest people leave small tasks to less-consuming minds. Learning how to delegate is the most important attribute of creating a company, and you must have people ready to pick up the slack. Like buckets gathering water, stress can overflow just one bucket, but if you have more than one bucket, the stress load becomes easier to handle.

People can be used to relieve stress. They can take on the stress of worrying about certain things and being concerned about other things. To take on a task on your own is to be selfish, misguided, and foolhardy. Use people—if they want to be used—to satisfy your need to get ahead. Apply their expertise in your field and build a system of people who can handle the stress when you cannot. If they cannot handle it, find people to help them handle their stress. The chain continues until there is no concern about completing anything. You can finish what you started.

STRUCTURE

Structure is the arrangement or relationship between the parts or elements of something complex. It gives a pattern to an organization. The most essential piece of any construction project is how it is structured. The thoughts, ideas, and buildings need structure.

The structure of everything in your life will determine how it functions. Everything in your existence has a structure. To maximize performance, you must know the structure inside out. You must know the DNA, components, and mechanisms. How you mesh and mold something will determine how your baby takes shape. Any project or creations that leave your mind or body should be considered a baby that needs care and concern. Take your time in creating something special. There is no rush. You still need experience to see what is wrong.

Stress for a building is wind and other elements. Stress for a car is driving. Stress for an idea is testing to see if the idea is possible. Anything you think of can become a reality—but not before testing it. When something is created around you, make sure you know the structure of it. In business, this will make you or break you. A bad foundation will sink and crumble from within. Take your time when building the foundation. You can move quicker in other decisions, but take your time with the floor be as precise as possible. Don't stress over things like that. When building something, build it as if it were a version of you. What would you look like and behave like if you were a building, a business, a vehicle, or an animal?

SUBCONSCIOUS

The subconscious is the part of the mind of which one is not fully aware, but it influences one's actions and feelings. It is the most powerful element of human existence because it is a stream of energy in the mind that never stops moving. Good thoughts, bad thoughts, and whatever you conceive will flow in the stream. The stream changes colors, density, and direction based on what you say and think.

It is important to pay close attention to what you put into your mind. Try to control how you feel about something. If you fear slipping on ice, remove it from the mind. Otherwise, you'll slip one day and not know why. You will learn about the subconscious throughout your life. The subconscious never turns off. Even while you sleep, it continues to flow. It sometimes projects images in your mind while you sleep.

Respect the mind, and the mind will open doors that you are unaware of. Respect your ways of thinking. For days on end, I was imagining a bird flying into the window over the kitchen sink. I kept telling myself that a bird would hit the glass one day. A year later, a bird hit the glass. From that moment on, I knew the power of the mind. The mind can make things happen. Fear is a strong influencer because it repeats itself in the mind. For the sake of what you are trying to build, you must remain positive. Remove any elements that might change that. Get rid of all bad vibes immediately.

SUCCESS IS GETTING WHAT YOU WANT—HAPPINESS IS WANTING WHAT YOU GET

If you want a really big house, success might mean getting a house. Happiness is getting a big house. Success might be getting the pair of shoes you want. Happiness is a new pair of designer shoes. Succeeding at something and doing something that makes you happy are different. Sometimes succeeding means obtaining something. At other times, a total victory means happiness. Happiness can be the result of trying to succeed.

The best way to go about life is to always be happy and geared toward gaining success. You can never go wrong if you're always in a happy mood—even when things don't go your way. Since unhappy situations will occur during the process, try to be happy all the time. Success comes to everyone who appreciates the journey. In life, the greatest assets you can have are happy thoughts and a clear mind. Aim for success in everything you do, but be happy when you fail. You are going to fail—even if your only failure is that you never failed. Being happy is the same thing. Even if nothing in your life goes the way you want it to, you can have a life of complete happiness. The most miserable people are successful people with no happiness. They claim that succeeding without being happy brings depression. Watch how you behave and feel toward yourself and others. If there is a choice between being happy and having success, choose wisely because one can definitely affect the other.

TAKE A CHANCE

Try saying yes to all opportunities. If you are scared, it is just insecurity. Picture walking outside in a heavy snowstorm. If you sit still too long, the snow begins to stick to you. When you reach your destination, you kick your feet and shake the snow off your shoulders. That is what it's like when you sit around and let insecurity settle on you. The layers of doubt and deceit begin to take hold of your mind, and before you know it, the opportunity to do anything is gone. Say yes! Even if it doesn't work out for you, the experience is what counts. There is nothing that can't be achieved. Why block yourself from glory? That is the only reason you don't have what you seek. You deserve the victory. Take what is yours. Go for it. What do you have to lose? You have so much to gain.

TAKE FIVE SECONDS

During a small decision, some people get lost in the sauce. They are puzzled about their next move and don't know what they should do. Do you want to post something online? On social media, do you use bad language to correct someone? Perhaps you want to blink out on your boss for not giving you enough vacation time. What if your favorite restaurant gives you a bad meal? Count to five and step outside of your body. Look yourself up and down, come back, and start over. You can figure out what you should do.

    Whenever you disagree with something, count backward from five. This separates you from the situation and gives you time to think about things from a different perspective. This simple gesture gives you an opportunity to determine what really happened and what can be done about it. Learn to step outside your mind and body to evaluate the situation. Count up to five for a decision—and count down from five for a situation.

TAKE NO CHANCES

It's better to be absolutely sure of something than to be unsure, especially with people. How can you be unsure of a person you don't know? That is too much of a risk to take. You will have to be the bearer of bad news someday. In cultivating a group of perfection, you would be a fool to think everyone you meet will be a trustworthy friend. When it's time to go, it's time to go. Don't prolong the goal of removing people you can no longer trust in your life, especially if the people you don't want to remain in your circle keep making the same mistakes. Forgive yourself for trusting that person. Be your own friend. In the end, you are your only friend. Why leave that job to others? Something or someone will let you down, but if you put faith in yourself, the pressure won't be as severe. Don't take chances with people who have proven themselves unworthy of your trust. That's like hugging a cactus and hoping it doesn't prick you. Always have a solution to remove people. Limit their tasks in case things go wrong. Even if nothing ever goes wrong, you want to have contingencies in place. Think of it as a spare tire in your special success car.

TAKING STEPS

Break everything down into manageable steps to reach a new plateau. One step should lead to the next like a staircase to your dreams. You might bump your head and miss a few steps along the way. No matter what, continue to climb those stairs. Too many people get distracted. They spend too much time caring about what others think. Fuck that. Do it for you—and you alone. By the time you get a quarter of the way toward your goal, you should be high enough where if you fall down the stairs, a bone would break. That is how high your goal should be. If you were walking down the highway, if you stopped, you would starve or die of thirst.

From this moment on, you are on a march. Rain, sleet, snow, or shine, you are on a march to the top. Every time your foot hits the ground, the world shakes and trembles at your movement. You are a giant walking casually toward a better tomorrow. Anyone who doesn't like you can do nothing to stop you. It doesn't matter if they put up roadblocks, build fortresses, or use elite attack helicopters. You are the giant they never saw coming, and they will never defeat you.

TARGETING

You should always be aiming at the most valuable when approaching prey. Like in a video game, you want the thing with the most points. It doesn't matter if it's a person, place, or thing. If the reward you receive is not worth the effort, move on. It doesn't matter how pretty someone is, how nice someone seems, or how close someplace is. Aim high, aim big, or don't aim at all. You better know the habits, thoughts, pleasures, and pains of the person you are after. You should know just about everything in the mind of the individual you're after. Make sure you pick the appropriate target. Don't waste your time if the benefit of acquiring the right person in your life is not worth the trouble. Many times, we go after the shiniest objects, and in most cases, that doesn't make it a noble cause. Like a robot that can get the diagnostics of anything it looks at, you should be able to tell whether the person, place, or object you seek is going to pay off the way it is supposed to. That is why it's best to take your time. Animals in the wild watch their prey for days before attacking. After they learn the nature of their victim, it is easier to strike a second or third time. If you have trouble choosing people, determine what you love to do with you time and what person, place, or thing can help you most.

THE BIGGEST THREAT TO YOUR LIFE IS PEOPLE

While writing this book, so many things occurred: fees, purchases, arguments, betrayals, deceptions, lies, false truths, backstabbing, accomplishments, goals, triumphs, relationships, and burned bridges. Much came from the simple fact that I spoke too much about my ambitions. I claimed too much to conquer and gave away too much information. Nobody really wants to see you succeed, and nobody wants you to do better than them. You would have to be a fool to believe you have friends with a bit of caution. People want to help you win—as long as they can control you or come along for the ride.

On the elite level, honest, genuine people are few and far between. Be wise in who you trust. Don't burden yourself or others with knowing too much of your ambition. Love everyone—but know that you should avoid some people. When you tell everyone everything, it can be taken as an insult to their ambition. Rather than being the loudmouth in the room, be quiet and observe people. You can't do anything without the help of others, and the most dangerous threat to you and your dreams come from people who are close to you.

People are as only as good as their capabilities. Some people can be counselors, and others can be partygoers. Most of the time, professionals should be held in high regard. Avoid mixing personal and business relationships. If you are interested in a family-owned business, be cautious because everyone gets along when the money comes in. Some family members might want to settle, and others might want to go higher. Everybody has different goals in life, and it is not wise to try to alter it. Focus on you. Let in those who want to be a part of your life—and move away from those who do not. Don't get caught up in attraction and value of people because everyone is replaceable, including you. Be kind. Take your time in appraising friendships, trust, and employment. You only have so many people to choose from. Don't point to the entire crowd and misjudge a few people without properly filtering their dreams and ambitions. Tossing people back into the pool might result in other people being contaminated with bad information. One bad apple can spoil the bunch.

THE SAME TACTICS

Once you have mastered the strategies and expertise required to thrive, it comes down to who else does the same thing. Enemies from the past will resurface and join forces with your current enemies. As long as you have tight grip on your life and business, they will only get so far. Just because different people join together against you doesn't mean they have the same tactics. Why would people join forces to attack you? They are trying to bring about your destruction.

When people team up, they should perform better. In the case of infiltrating or sabotaging your success, multiple minds cannot defeat you. It's all in the mind. Many people will try to hurt you. That is an indication that you are close to finish line. The enemy tries to outsmart you, but they cannot outthink you. They will be developing tactics against you. They will do the same things over and over, which is a great way to recognize a new enemy. They will do the same things you've experienced before, and you will recognize their motives and intentions before they reach the first phase of attack. Pay close attention to the tactics and actions of people.

THE LESSER OF TWO EVILS

If you had a choice between someone you didn't like and someone you couldn't stand, which would you choose? Not every situation will work out in victory. You might have to compromise. Some people will try to take what's yours, and others will try to destroy you. Which is worse: an enemy trying to destroy you or an enemy trying to steal from you? Sometimes you are going to have to let things play out and return later to wrap things up. That is the difference between a battle and a war.

There are many different kinds of friction that will occur in life. Some will not be your fault, and others will be your fault. You are responsible for every outcome because you have control over how you react to things. Never let someone fool you into thinking you have to react immediately or in a certain way. Take your time to assess which part of the problem can remain until you have a better grip on the situation. Which person, place, or thing is heavier in the issues you face? When trying to decide what to eliminate first, choose whatever is most threatening to your future. Some things might linger, and others will be constant threats.

THE LORD HELPS THOSE WHO HELP THEMSELVES

Whether you are religious and believe in a higher power or are intuitive to the creation of life, there is a higher force at work. The universe is alive and moving toward a common goal of continuous evolution. It is not a simple matter of looking at the sky or any creation for guidance. It takes more than that. Asking for help without action is the same as taking proper nutrients but not working out. You have to contribute some effort. Nothing in the universe is free, and energy cannot be destroyed. It can only be transferred to something else. Respect the laws of nature, energy, life, attraction, and creation.

These universal laws are the reason for existence.

To be lazy and hope for the best is to be selfish and assume that life has more mercy on you than any other form of creation in the universe. Follow the steps to a better understanding of what it means to exist—and form a strategy to better yourself and those around you. You are a unique individual, and your gift is the ability to be different. The most important weapon in your arsenal is the change you can make for yourself. You will face plenty of uncontrollable problems. You have to offer it up to a higher power, and you also have to contemplate why the problems exist for you. Every failure or attempt at success will be a lesson for you. Most of these lessons come in the form of problems. It is up to you to decipher what to take from every encounter in your journey.

THE REAL WORLD

What you seek isn't always what you thought it was. Some things are worth the thrill. Most stuff isn't a big deal. Do not take pride in trivial items like shoes or purses. Diamonds are different topic because they represent the struggle for some people and are used as a symbol of success. Take pride in land, houses, art, and awards. They will appreciate in value. Imagine if you already had what you seek. What would your attitude be? You would just seek the next item or goal. Maintain your thought process before you obtain anything. You will realize the importance of a consistent way of living. Nothing is ever like it seems, and everything that glitters isn't gold. Sugar and salt appear the same until you taste them. The things you wish to receive will not be as fancy as they appear. Don't be swept off your feet only to be disappointed later.

THE WORST IS BEHIND YOU

Once you are able to put things behind you, keep them there. When the issue passes you by, put it behind you. Change your ways, change your habits, and change everything you can change. Maneuver around the bullshit—and keep it away from you. Once those people are removed, keep them in the rearview mirror. Learn to embrace everything that occurs—good and bad—but continue to move forward. When you go past an object, it can't come back to hit you in the back. Picture yourself passing a car on the highway. The car has two choices: hitting you on the side or speeding up and hitting you from behind. Don't slow down and let the problem catch up to you. Don't stop. Keep moving, grooving, and letting the progress flow.

Holding on to a loss from a struggle you have suffered is never worth it. Learn to let certain shit go. You can dwell on something bad happening to you and do something about it at the same time. It happened. Let it go, move on, and find a solution. If there is no solution, keep moving. You're on a journey, and tripping, falling, and stumbling are part of the process.

THE WORST THINGS NEVER HAPPEN

Exaggerating is the best thing anyone can do for publicity. Don't believe the hype. If it doesn't apply, let it fly. Controversy, sales, and causing friction between opposing factions is what most people do best. Don't believe any of what you hear or see. You can only control your reactions and responses. Why care? He said, she said is the world's greatest deceiver. Finding someone who really cares is rare, and that is why you have to stay close to what you believe in. Unless the threat of what you fear kills you, do not worry about it. Let it go. Your life is better viewed through your own lens. Keep your eyes on the prize—and look to future victories. Bad thoughts are the biggest enemy, but they are a sign of progress. If your mind has the ability to conceive of bad scenarios, put an end to the madness by appreciating the fact that such scenarios exist in the first place.

THINGS REVEAL THEMSELVES

When people die, you sometimes learn more about them than when they were alive. You can learn a lot about a person from the people they touched, the places they've been, and the accomplishments they have made. People get caught up in materialistic things and don't focus on the history and memories that can be made. When you leave the world and travel to the great beyond, what do you want to be said about you? Is it something you've done with your life or a goal you reached? Be observant about what will last after you are gone. You are only here for a short amount of time, and you don't want it to be spent being angry and frustrated about what you did or didn't do with your life.

If you want to know about a person who has passed, look at what they left behind. If they left something behind, they have companions who can speak to their favor. You can't build anything alone except a pile of shit, and even then, someone has to clean it up. Don't be selfish in your ambitions. Don't be blindsided by the notion that everyone will be coming with you to the top.

Prepare for the future and set aside a little for your grandchildren. The best things are things you deserve. Imagine the joy of helping your grandchildren with an inheritance. They will look at your history, follow in your footsteps, and emulate your ambition. They will revel in the past, relive your journey, and read about what you have done. Whatever the case, you can be a gift for generations to come. Plan ahead, focus, and work hard. Don't fret over minor losses that will be forgotten.

THINKING IS SYSTEMATIC—AND CONVERSATION IS MECHANICAL

Every time you come up with an idea, a system should be put in place to run and sustain it properly. Your mind should function like a computer. How will the goal be reached? What functions will sustain it? The formation of what you want to build is the main concern at all times—even in the grocery store. Where does a product come from? How it is created? How is it shipped? In conversations with people, it's all about the technique. Conversing with people is like a tennis ball; it's a give and take. You want to exhaust your opponent before putting them down for the count. Not every challenge you face will require the immediate defeat of an opponent. When trying to score a date, you better play the smart game. It's easy to communicate with people, but you need to understand who you are talking to.

With some confidence, you should be able to talk to anybody—even if you have to talk to yourself. Altering your mind to see the functionality in everything that moves and appears before your eyes will be tough, but once you master it, things become easy. You will see function in everything you look at. An astronaut sees the possibilities of going in space, and a scuba diver sees the same thing underwater.

THIRD EYE

Everyone has a third eye. It is above the nose and between the eyes. It is the truth, the unbelievable truth, and the undeniable truth. This world is ugly, and the things that go on every day will make you sick to your stomach. It's best to accept that what you see in the mirror on the way up will not be the same on your return. The ugliness will rub off on you and become a part of your texture. Let go of what you think is good and just and see that powerful people run everything. You feed on the crumbs that fall from their tables until you are capable enough to do what you need to do. Be the biggest threat to the system that you can be. Patience is key before you release your inner strength. Accept the truth about the world and adapt to it. Timing is key to escaping the muddy bottom of the barrel. That is where the most action happens, and you will earn your stripes there. If you are not willing to do what it takes to get to a better way of living, don't complain about being there. You're only going to ruin it for everyone else. You will have to get a little dirty before you can see the light. Don't be fooled. The most beautiful flowers can have the biggest thorns and be the most poisonous. Let the venom soak into your skin, build in your body, and change you. It will alter your appearance to match the deception. If you become a fast talker, dress to impress and use the gift of gab. You know how to have fun. You know how to look the part. You know how to invite a confrontation. Some asses will get kicked, but no one needs to see you practicing field goals in private.

TIME MAXIMIZATION

In this form of production, you do multiple things at the same time. The most effective method is overlapping different ventures. While attending college, I am buying licenses for my business. These menial tasks coincide with each other. The business helps the book, the book helps school, and school helps the business. Like a wheel turning, they contribute to one another.

The most important thing is to add a little bit to each one every day. Your goals have to be different and have different demands to maximize your time. You can't do the same thing every day and hope to make a difference. It has to be multiple things—preferably three small tasks that go along with each other—that are related but not in the same field. They contribute to each other and work cohesively.

If one skill fails, the others can keep going—eventually pulling along the one job you couldn't handle alone. Opposites attract. Use that to your advantage by mixing and matching your goals. Set aside time to execute a separate mission for each one. It can be effective to use your time and money to reach a goal. It's up to you to perceive the information. When going after your goals, there is a way to do everything properly and efficiently.

TIMELY FASHION

Sometimes untimely things work out in your favor. Patience is the only thing that will get you through times of hardship. Some things occur at the worst possible moments and ruin everything. You can flip that. You can turn simple opportunities into moments of grandeur. If you are late to a graduation, it is not the end of the world. During the ceremony, stop and pick up some flowers.

If you are patient and confident, you can improve any moment. Concentration and attention can get you throughout any ordeal. Never panic when something doesn't go your way. The first defeat is losing sight of a victory in times of stress. Use being late, the absence of time, and fatigue to your advantage. The biggest names in investing made their fortunes during times of peril. They saw opportunities in the market before major shifts.

Every tragedy has a bounce-back period. You must recognize what's missing and supply it before someone else does. If you are late for a date, turn it into the most romantic night ever. All you have to do is come up with a way to turn the frustration into entertainment, stimulation, and amusement. It's up to you to turn time into a weapon. Time is a weapon because we all have a limited amount of it. Use it wisely during connections. If you want to meet someone, show up at two events. Manipulate the circumstances a little bit and make yourself more interesting.

THE KAIZEN PRINCIPLE

The Kaizen principle can change your life completely because it makes you realize your potential. Do one more thing than you did the day before. It could be a range of intricate things that seem simple, but when added together, the potential for completing a task is much greater.

In a typical day, you might you wake up, eat breakfast, do your chores, go to work, come home, cook dinner, exercise, and then sleep. With the Kaizen principle, you do the same activities, but you add one more task the next day. You might read a book for thirty minutes. The next day, add reading for an hour. The next day, add doing your laundry.

It doesn't matter what you add and take away as long as the routine is consistent. You will end up booking your entire day with small activities that correlate to one another. Have a maximum of ten, and when one is completed, replace it with two new ones. You don't have to do major tasks every day because small objectives add up to a major task.

Consistency is the key to moving forward. To build momentum, set up small-ticket items that go with one another. If one doesn't get done, two doesn't get done. After doing laundry, plan the next day's activities. Stay ahead of your schedule—and always do one more thing than the day before. It doesn't have to be anything major, but it must contribute to your projects.

TRUST IN YOUR ENEMY'S HATRED

When people show you their true colors, believe them. Don't just stand there. Run for it. You don't need to be friends or associates with anyone who misconstrues your message, talks bad about you, or disrespects you. One incident is bad enough. It could be jealousy, envy, or pride. They might not like you. Trust their hatred. The disbelief of someone's betrayal can lead to making that person love you or care about you.

It might be a grave shock, but you can let it go. If you take care of yourself and properly evaluate people, one or two misjudgments won't hurt you. The way someone looks at you is a great indicator of the concern they have for you. When you know someone is your enemy, trust them to let you know it at every turn.

They will always try to take a piece of you. They will use words and phrases to damage your ego because they know you are watching or listening to them. Your reputation is the most vital asset. Seeing poisonous people in your presence can't taint your judgment of character.

Don't let a proven traitor hang around you without some serious investigation. Once you recognize that someone doesn't like you, don't waste your time trying to get to know them. Do you see zebras trying to get to know lions? Predators and prey can become friends in controlled environments. People are the same way. If a bigger person won't intervene and set things straight, don't bother. You have to watch everybody and keep up your guard. The enemy's goal is to remain around you. Without that, they have to move on to other prey.

TRUST IS A BRIDGE

Trust is the most valuable asset in the history of mankind, and it is the most underrated and abused artifact ever created. Since the dawn of humanity, trust has been the key to survival. Trust has been the reason for humankind making it this long. Construction, organization, agriculture, defense systems, attack strategies, flight transition, animal control, and education are tools we use every day to grow and nurture society.

Trust is important for establishing balance and getting things done. When you cross a bridge, you trust the architect to make sure nothing collapses. When you shake someone's hand, you trust they will do something. What about the contract you signed? Does that person really have to abide by it? In most cases, yes. In more aggressive circumstances, forces are a necessity. Don't fall prey to that requirement. If you have to use force to solve a problem, you double your chances of failure. The only real connection is trust. Animals trust each other to help when necessary.

Animals of the same species sometimes harm each other. That's the way life is. It doesn't mean we're doomed, but we should take precaution in our movements. If this world was entirely trustworthy, insurance wouldn't exist. Courts and law enforcement would be unnecessary. Unfortunately, we live in a world where trust can be broken. Accidents happen, and people make mistakes. Trust is so important. If trust is broken—so is the connection. You can't cross a broken bridge. Don't put too much stress on the trust you've established with someone. You wouldn't want things to collapse, would you?

UGLY PEOPLE DO UGLY THINGS

Never focus on the appearance of people when trying to judge their character. Go completely off of their actions. It's okay to be cool with someone. It's even okay to call them an associate, but a friend, business partner, family member is not a light term to play with. Before you allow someone into your inner circle, you should put them through the wringer. Make sure they qualify before adding them to the group. Some of the worst actions come from the best intentions. Don't get played. Before you look to the outside, examine yourself on the inside. Evaluate your personality and see what makes you tick. How easily can you be broken down? What triggers you? These are the components to get control of before seeking anyone's company. Not everyone mixes, opposites attract, and the most compatible people might not have the appearance you want.

Nice-looking people can associate with people who don't look as good and still get the job done together. Don't be vexed when an attractive person does something wrong or corrupt. Many people like that have a history of doing bad things. They are little messed up in the mind because the shiniest objects get the most attention. People who are exposed to too much attention become addicted to it. Some even abuse it. Don't be surprised when the ugliness of their nature is revealed. A rosebush will fuck you up if you are not careful. "Look—but don't touch—buddy." People with a tendency to do wrong may present themselves as good people. Don't get caught up in their psychological defects. Looks can be deceiving—even in calm, controlled environments.

UNDER-PROMISE AND OVERDELIVER

Not everyone loves surprises. When people say they don't like surprises, they are referring to a primitive version of a surprise—like loud noises or rambunctious environments. A surprise party always involves loud noise. We tend to recognize the shock that comes with a little stimulation. A party might be full of loving, cherished people, but the shock of being surprised can be overwhelming.

At a party, friends and family may pay tribute and exchange hugs and kisses, but that's about it. What if you could give more than that? People's expectations are being altered by their actions. Instead of just giving the person you care about a physical thrill, give them a mental one too. When you under-promise and overdeliver, you set a bar for yourself. Once that bar has been set, you can surprise the person with more than they bargained for.

Start with a mediocre expectation—a small promise one you can do at the moment—and remain fully aware of it. You can focus on building an even bigger award. You may want to get your lover a gift like a bag or a shirt. When you then retrieve the gift, give them a belt, a second bag, or a coat. That is compounding the interest.

Doubling the stimulation should end with the result being confusion about where to start. The person being awarded should be confused about the nature of why you did something in the first place. A two-for-one deal doesn't have to be material things. It could be favors or a mixture of both. The more points you tap in that box of the mind, the better stimulation and the better memories you can create. It is great to see your good work on a daily basis.

URGES

Women are the most dangerous element in the world. They have the strength to control their urges. You can talk a girl into anything if you have the skill, but it takes time for them to warm up to you. Women are like volume buttons, and men are like light switches. You have to take your time and get the right frequency. What you sacrifice is time and patience. This is how a walk in the park late at night turns into something else. A little charm, good tact, and patience create the perfect mixture. You wouldn't have to work so hard if she was easy. Would you want her if she was that easy?

If first place was easy to get, would you want it? If second place was easy to get, would you want it? Women can control some things, and there are men who have mastered their urges and desires. For some reason, it is easier for females to hide. You have to master your urges. It doesn't have to be a date or recreational pleasure. While being yelled at or disrespected, the urge to respond or react will be greatest. Ask yourself if the energy you are going to expel is going to be worth it. The only way you are going to get ahead is if you focus what you comes from your being while in the process of succeeding. Nothing else matters if you can control yourself and most of the things around you.

UPGRADE

An upgrade is an improvement on something. The best advantage of an upgrade is the ability to avoid staying in the same place. Imagine someone stealing an idea or an item you were working on. They only have the first building stages. They still need to complete the idea or creation in order for it to live up to its potential.

At a certain point, people will begin to follow you. They want to sabotage and confiscate your creations, but it doesn't really matter because they only took the unfinished product. Within your brilliant mind, you have the ability to finish what you started. All you have to do is be smart and continue on the journey.

Like an animal that really loves you, what someone takes from you can only be allowed by what you create. What you create and build will always work in your favor, especially if it comes from a place of love. Nothing that loves you will ever betray you—no matter how bad it seems. If someone stole your car, the smartest thing you can do is use a tracker. Another way to protect yourself is to always have a contingency plan. In case of an emergency, you might have to destroy your beloved property and start over.

Be prepared for the worst—but hope for the best. Upgrade yourself. You can't be moving into a different way of life while conducting the same hobbies. All of us should master reading and writing before moving up the ladder of success. Your dress and performance speak volumes when you cannot. Be wise and smart in your wishes. When you look in the mirror, a rich and fully loaded version should be looking back at you. You should always love what you see in the mirror, and you should always seek to improve your mind and appearance. The best version of you likes little of what you used to like and has a better version of the indulgences you enjoy.

VIOLENCE

Violence is physical force intended to hurt, damage, or kill someone or something. Some people need their asses kicked to function, and that is something that should be your concern. You don't have to harm anyone to convince them to do as they are told. Violence can be found in all forms of media, education, and culture. You should be capable of doing something to anyone if necessary. You are the arms and legs of what you create. If backing up threats by using a different form of communication is required, then that is the way things are.

You go out at night to get some food, start up the car, earn the money, spend the money, and make sure gas is in the vehicle. What if you are on the way to someone's house and decide you might hurt them if they disagree with you? This is unhealthy. During the conversation, the person starts a confrontation. You decide to hurt the person and leave. That is the end of it. It is like going out at night to get food. It goes easily, and there are no mishaps along the way. Unfortunately, going out for food at night is the same as going to someone's house, hurting them, and leaving.

You might have to hurt someone and move on in life. You might never get violent, but destroying them will take more than words. You must be willing to go far enough to get your point across and protect your ambitions. If possible, take up martial arts or self-defense and learn the basics of combat. This will train your mind to remain calm. The training you receive will give you confidence in your defense capabilities.

VICES

You can deny habits, bad nature, drives, and motivations, but you cannot control them. These are the things that determine your success in the future. Your habits will alter the routine of your ambitions. A vice is immoral or wicked behavior, but most people relate it to something you like to do for pleasure. Smoking is a vice that most people would refer to as a health hazard. The human mind develops an addiction to whatever stimulates it. That's why people enjoy getting tattoos, which is a form of torture. Tattoos are interesting, but it involves some questionable characteristics.

Having control is important with vices. Drug addiction is a form of self-poisoning. If not curtailed, these habits are like unwanted people. Smoking can be a monkey on your back, and the urges can be out of control. There is a constant need for stimulation, and it has no stop button. It constantly attacks the mind and strains the denial muscles. Eventually, you surrender to take the edge off. You must build stronger muscles by working out the areas you are weakest. A porn addiction can be helped via methods that remove the thought of such materials. Exercises can prevent people from indulging in such behavior. It may take practice or professional help, but if you don't learn to control yourself around unsafe things you enjoy, you are putting your life in jeopardy.

VIBES

Vibes are a person's emotional state or the atmosphere of a place as communicated to and felt by others. This is a psychedelic way of thinking. The best way to stay in tune is to make people think about those who did you wrong. Would they like you being around them today? Would their speech patterns, ideas, and movements annoy you or cause you discomfort?

A lot of people do the same things, and nothing is new under the sun. This person could be a bad choice to be around. Some people put on a front when meeting you even though they might have good intentions for you. They might give off little signs that they are not good for you. You can apply this knowledge to see if people are who they say they are.

You will notice the behaviors of people when you compare them to one another. The recognition might cause you to be mad or upset at first. Some of the greatest relationships become tainted when you realize people's underhanded tactics. Intuition is the greatest tool when approaching people because people tend to do the same things in different ways.

VOICES

The narrator in your mind has to shut the hell up. Force your mind to gain control of your thoughts or risk becoming a victim. Behave as if someone is constantly reading your thoughts. Your adult thoughts don't have to be silenced, but you should control how they come and what they do when you create new ones. This world has many delights to offer, and your mind needs to develop a shell to remain focused. Tell yourself to shut up when it is important to control unneeded thoughts. Think about how you feel. You always have a voice in your head, and you have to be smart to control it. Build an anti-voice to tell yourself the right and wrong things to do. This thought process accepts whatever comes to mind. Keep your inner voice in check—but let it out every once in a while. Don't fall prey to the selfish urges you naturally develop.

WEAPONRY

Learn how to form weapons from thin air. A weapon is a means of gaining an advantage or defending oneself in a conflict or contest. You can use different forms of weapons on those you disagree with. Be prepared to use them. Practice is important for using a weapon against anything threatening you. You want to be as accurate and precise.

Be ready to make a weapon out of anything you can get your hands on. The most sophisticated weapons are the ones that come from knowledge. Knowledge and patience are the only proper alternatives to great skills. Understanding who and what the problem is and what you need to take them down is important for maintaining balance.

When it's time to take someone down, use every force possible to manifest something that will give you power over whatever threatens you. You don't want to find yourself on the losing end of a battle you could've won with proper analysis of the situation.

WE ARE SLAVES OF OURSELVES

You will always win—and you will always lose at the exact same time. This statement is the purest form of the absolute truth. It doesn't have to be free speech, but your words should never affect the minds and hearts of others without your permission. You can't say what you want—even when you are supposed to say it. Words are nothing more than sounds as air leaves the body, but words are the leading cause of everything around you. Somebody had to give instruction to the builders, and they listened to the architect, and they listened to the teacher.

More bloodshed has come as a result of words than actions. You always have a chance to speak about anything you disagree with. Even if the outcome will be the same, you are still given the final word. Actions have their own way of creeping up on us. Words are manageable, but they get us in the most trouble. The easiest things are the most attractive and get done first.

You will not be swayed by trivial matters. When it's time to be quiet, you will be quiet. When it's time to speak, you can use your words. When you are pushed to anger, you will refrain from speaking.

WHAT DOESN'T KILL YOU MAKES YOU STRONGER

After an extended period of time, a broken bone repairs itself. Bone is a distant cousin of rock. The bone's cells and marrow are used maintain rigidity and hardness. Over time, bones deteriorate, which causes pains and aches. Some pains come prematurely due to many things, including bad nutrition.

On a cellular level, our bones have webs. The webs are the foundations of the bones. Bones are made up of many things and have a way of repairing themselves. When the bone breaks, that is when the magic happens. Many people fail to realize that the bone actually hardens to prevent itself from breaking in the same spot again. The details are in the webs. As the bones repair, the webs reconnect like plugs and sockets. They add more layers to the web and thicken. This is how martial artists get harder bones. They kick trees and bamboo until the nerves in the shin die. This exercise makes the legs harder and more durable.

Many martial artists have deadly techniques from simple maneuvers. They've beaten themselves up so much their bodies have become extremely tough. The body thinks it's being attacked repeatedly, and it effectively hardens that area to provide more strength. If a professional martial artist kicks an average person in the leg, the martial artist will not be hurt. His or her body is too strong to put down. In this universe, you have to be tough and resilient to make it. Too much energy is put into complaining about how much things hurt. You need to absorb that pain and let it build you into something stronger. No pain, no gain.

WHAT YOU CHASE ELUDES YOU

Whatever you want most is always out of reach. A complete picture generally is what people tend to be after, and the majority of the time, they never achieve it. If it were up to humankind, we would all be flying around with superpowers, everyone would be rich, and no one would fail. As life would have it, that will never be the case. The world will never be perfect in any shape or form. This is not being cynical. It is being truthful.

In a perfect world, pollution wouldn't exist. In a balanced world, pollution would have time to go away and dissipate. That makes the dream of perfection a nonreality because mistakes always need time to heal. Hunger will never go away, and problems will continue to exist. To assume all will be perfect is unfair. There will never be a perfect time to do anything. Take advantage of that and go for whatever you seek at all times.

The things you want will keep their distance from you. If it's a lover you seek, when you obtain the necessary features that might attract this person, you will come to know yourself differently than when you began. Discovering that person might or might not have been worth the journey. This will be evident if you catch that person. You might not like the person in the wedding picture. You might not like your reflection in the mirror after having an intimate moment of heated passion. You might not like your personality.

Don't get caught in the allure of something only to discover you were attracted to the appearance of something. That is why buying a car is more satisfying when you can test-drive it first. You will know if it's worth it or not. You can change the color and add or subtract things you don't like. You can do this with a lot of material things. With people, it isn't the same. You can't just alter someone. You will always be chasing that person—whether you are getting into a relationship or maintaining a relationship. What you chase will always elude you.

Attracting people is different. It requires much more mental energy, and to some degree, you must remain stationary. You may be chasing the appearance of someone you want to keep following you. Remain in control by attracting what you like and doing whatever is necessary to make your desires stay.

WHAT YOU SEE IS WHAT YOU GET

If it walks like a duck, talks like a duck, and quacks like a duck, it's a duck. If it's a platypus, then it's something special. Most of the time, whatever you encounter is pretty much what it is. Deception is when you feel as though you are being tricked, but that might not be the case. Your eyes can fool you sometimes. It's hard to trust anything you see because the camera is a liar.

Most of television isn't true, and it's hard to trust visuals, but the context of how it makes you feel is pretty simple. Most of the time, you have to be completely aware of the situation you are getting yourself into. If you are sitting still in a room with one chair and no windows, and then somebody walks in the room, whose fault is it if something bad happens? Keep your guard up at all times. Everyone has a motive, and if they want to interact with you, you have full control of your surroundings. Make sure you have full disclosure about what is going on around you. If a snake shows itself, you know there are no rats around you. It might bite you—but what provoked it? You see it for what it is. Why is it around? A gardener knows about bugs, a driver knows about mechanics, and a chef knows about food. Why would a snake show up around you?

All people have a purpose. Some are troublemakers. You can easily spot this if you know what to look for. You can recognize when something goes wrong and who might be at fault. If you don't have experience, that is fine. As long as the big picture is in focus, variations will be easy to spot. If someone comes around you, ask yourself what they are up to.

WHEN THE GOING GETS TOUGH, DIG DEEP

This is the best time to get excited. At moments like this, the situation means well for you. Like getting rid of a stain in your clothing, sometimes ridding yourself of the bad includes a little fading of the original appearance. Retreating to safety to gather your thoughts is not a cowardly move. Never look at yourself as a failure because you got out of Dodge when the shit hit the fan.

To win wars, you need to lose a couple battles. A coordinated loss will work better in controlling a situation. Your enemies will follow the path you set for them. Have faith in your ability to remove yourself from a conflict that is not going in your favor. The people who you don't want in your life—and the things you don't need in it—are shedding themselves from your existence.

People can be so jealous and envious of you that they all try to gang up on you the second you are about to change your life. Picture everyone as arrows surrounding you. They are pushing and pointing toward you. It's a good sign that things are meant to happen the way they are. To dig in deep, you must study harder, research harder, and work harder. Harder is the key. Do not shift and take the easy route. Buy more books, supplies, and investments. It's not a luxury to leave a situation you can't control. You have to pause—but do not take a vacation or focus on anything else. Give the extra effort and pay attention to whatever needs your attention.

WHAT DO THEY KNOW?

The information you have must be kept sacred. Your enemies will attack you on the levels you provide. If there is no information to give anyone, they will never know where you are coming from. If your enemy realizes the information you have, you can reveal your weaknesses. You shoot three-pointers, they're coming in for a block and a layup. Kickboxers uses martial arts, and your enemies might use sticks, knives, or bats. Deep-sea divers need oxygen tanks. Your enemies might poke a hole in your tank before you submerge. A NASCAR driver might receive a flat tire before a race. It's always going to depend on what you know and share with others. The safest way to go about it is to keep all your information confidential. Be careful about the information you have and what you displayed to others. Most times, you can tell what their intentions are.

WHISPERS OF LIGHT

Listen close and listen well. do you hear your thoughts and the ideas of what you must do today? All these things on your mind— the excitement of going out tonight, the fun you're going to have on vacation, the tasty food you're going to enjoy for dinner—are nothing but selfish ambition you feel you deserve because you exist.

What about the person who will not wake up tomorrow? What about the starving family that will lose a family member tonight? What about the untold wars and deaths? All you can think of is enjoying your day. Don't be foolish. You have no love in your heart if you don't do at least one good deed a week. For some, the most extreme thing would be doing something wonderful for someone else daily. Paying for the next person's coffee behind you is a start.

Every day, do something wonderful for someone else. No matter how big or small—just do it. Do not speak about it either. Never confess it. You will start working a positive energy muscle or spirit muscle in your body. This creates energy around you and attracts people to protect you. As you quiet down your mind and listen to the world, you will notice voices saying things to help you on your journey.

If you were to go to the market to buy an apple, the clerk might say, "I was looking to build my car and found information online." Someone else might say, "I found information about preventing forest fires or helping the less fortunate." This information might pertain you, and it might be an idea you haven't discovered yet.

People recognize those who are trying to do well, and after a while, they will contribute to the protection and safety of what you represent by offering you words of wisdom. Always keep an open ear to anyone who crosses your path. Whether you know it or not, someone is in need of what you are trying to succeed in. The small brief messages you hear along the way can lead you to the most glorious success. Help others, keep love in your heart, and love the idea that whatever you want to do in your life will help someone escape a dark place.

WISDOM OF ME

You should know exactly what goes on with you internally and externally: weight, height, TV settings, the average number of chips in your favorite bag. Every detail matters, and it is best to be on top of them. That way, any confusion or disruption will be caught quickly. As far as your crew or staff, you should know every detail and habit they have. Their problems, skills, and abilities are important. They should know you. A person, team, or company should move as an impenetrable unit. You should be aware of anything you say, do, or endorse at any given point. If it doesn't mix well with what you have going for yourself, avoid it. If it doesn't work, seek a different resolution by changing your habits, ways, or people around you. Know all your weaknesses before you know your strengths. Discover how to fix what holds you back from moving up. A drug dealer knew the cops had visited his stash house by noticing the lock was turned a few degrees. Sometimes you're going to have information and weapons that are stronger than the whole team, and that's okay. You can protect yourself and your team by withholding certain things until the last minute.

WITH GREAT POWER COMES GREAT RESPONSIBILITY

That famous superhero statement has a lot meaning. For starters, obtaining that kind of power is no easy task. Managing it is an ever-greater task. Power takes great responsibility.

    You worked so hard to get to the point where your opinion matters, and then someone tried to get you to do something that was not agreeable with you. The old you would have lashed out and said something, but the new you finds the act annoying and unsettling. This is the mind-set of someone who has grown and evolved.

There is probably someone in your life who you dislike. If you could, you would kick their ass with no problem. After not being around that person for a while, you find them less bothersome. This is the evolution of the self, and it is a reflection of growth and maturity. You possess a greater understanding of your potential and power.

After trying to accomplish so much, that person has not flourished. What do you do? Do you lose your temper and go off? No. Instead, you forgive them for their faults and move on. There is no merit in the destruction of someone who is not a threat. Don't take pride in teaching that person a lesson. Keeping moving forward. It is a sign that there something better for you. You have triumphed over annoying people.

Everyone has the power to follow the rules and control their attitudes. Great power is for people in politics, sports, or the military. After dealing with other people's problems, you learn a new perspective. Would you care about someone putting you down with the same old bullshit after you been through so much? Hurry up and evolve—so nothing fazes you anymore.

WORK WITH WHAT YOU HAVE

Many people seek help they can already find for themselves. All you have to do is look inward. Most of the problems you come across will be problems you have to face on your own. There might be opportunities for others to help, but they are still your problems. The ability to step outside the box and think of a solution is valuable when coming up with ways to fix a situation.

If your car breaks down on your way to work, that is your fault. You knew what type of car you were getting into. You also knew what would happen if a situation like that occurred. Even if that were the last thing to cross your mind, you still have to be prepared. Calm down. Is there a spare tire in the trunk? If you do not know how to change a tire, it is not a big deal. Flag someone down to help you change the tire. You carried yourself and helped yourself at the same time. You didn't panic, you found a solution, and you found a way to fix the problem by using someone else. Now you can laugh during lunch.

The key to finding inner strength is to never panic and always give yourself an out. Leave a trapdoor for someone to sneak in and help—or sneak out and help yourself. The trapdoor in the car was the spare in the trunk. It allowed a random person to intervene and save the day. Always be prepared and listen to your heart and your gut. If these things are telling you to get an extra pair of shoes, put a spare tire in the trunk, or keep a spare phone charger in the car, do it. Your intuition is guiding you. Your subconscious, intuition, gut feelings, and heart will guide you in preparing for the unknown. Never ignore them.

YOU ALWAYS HAVE A STORY

No matter what, there is always a story to tell. It doesn't have to be a major triumph or a major catastrophe, but there is always a story to tell. You should keep a journal or diary and write in it every day. Write down your dreams, problems, and adventures. Write down anything you can think of. Eventually you will have developed a story of your life. There is something in your life that is worth noting—and even the smallest events can turn into a story.

If you start paying attention to everything going on around you and stop being caught up in the moment, you will learn to accept and be thankful for everything that happens. When good things come your way, you will be more appreciative. Time waits for no one, and you are going to pass all kinds of beautiful things. These magnificent events won't last forever. Take note of the best things that happen to you and the not-so-great things that happen to you. You are guaranteed to laugh at the past once you get past it, but for a joyful personal experience, you will be even happier if you write it down and read it later. Do yourself a favor and begin making history by writing down a chapter of your life. Some of your encounters might be epic tales.

YOU CAN'T DO BOTH

You can't chase after two things at once. Have you ever seen a person catch two animals at the same time? Have seen a car go in two directions at the same time? Have you looked in two directions at the same time? You have to choose which one is more important— and go after it with all your heart. That is the only way to succeed. Otherwise, you will lose—and both goals will be lost. Select the one that produces the best outcome.

Don't think situations will align themselves all the time. More often than not, you will have to take down your prey one by one. One of the most important traits is patience. Waiting for an opportunity while chasing another will never be a problem for you again. Put your heart into all everything do—and make your shift at the right time. Never shift suddenly without proper justification, adaptation, and preparation.

YOU NEGOTIATE WHAT YOU GIVE

You get what you give. If people know they can give you ten and get back twenty, they will always give you what you are looking for and more. Never be greedy—and never take more than you need. Pay all of your debts. All debt is bad—don't take on any of it. There is no good name founded on owing someone else. If you owe somebody, pay up in full. The money will be there, and the opportunity will arise.

Your word carries a bond that your actions cannot carry all the time. A loan might be needed from time to time. Your presentation and admiration will get you in the door. How you perform is entirely up to you. Your instincts shouldn't let you down.

Don't tell anyone about your dream. Tell them about the motions you're conducting to get there. Like a train that's leaving with or without you, your job is to get as many people as possible to board. Be cautious about sharing money. No situation is ever perfect, but your attitude, tone, and texture will be.

YOUR ANGELS GUARD YOU—AND YOUR DEMONS FIGHT FOR YOU

A lot of people won't like you. A lot of people will like you. Know who you are dealing with. The angels will tell you when they defend you from harm—or you might see it for yourself. Demons will never be seen or heard, but their actions will be loud and clear. Their intent is to use you because they like you, your product, or your message. They do not want to help you and your ambitions. They could not care less if you make it or not. They know they have a better shot with you than someone else. They would rather not risk you being attacked by a force you can't control.

An angel will be the hero that does the right thing for a good result. Demons will the bad person who creates a bad result. They might even alter the way things turn out for you. If you are good at being a villain, they will take the chance of doing your bidding. Instead of calling the police, they might carry out your will in another way. That is why you need to be clear and precise.

Demons only want you around to feed off of you—and nothing more. They don't want anyone else feeding off of you. Angels want to invite as many people as they can and save as many as they can. Learn the difference between friends and family when pursuing your dream. Be clear about how you want things to get done and how you want things to run. Otherwise, you leave yourself open to reckless decisions.

ZERO FACTOR

When you focus, you will notice variations in your emotions. If something you're doing is bringing stress, continuing is up to you. If you are walking across the street, and the light turns green before you can make it to the other side, you'd want to hurry up. Nobody wants to get hit by car. If you look both ways and hurry across before oncoming traffic catches you, your senses spike and become more in tune with your surroundings. This might take place without you even knowing.

If you feel the same way around certain individuals, something is wrong. Perhaps you want that person to help you out, but it takes away from your peace of mind. People can be obstacles and cause you to take detours. You are always on a path—whether you are sitting perfectly still or playing basketball. Your life is always on a path, and the people you allow into your life with either try to get you off of that path or help you stay on it.

Removing all stresses will help you zero in on who or what is causing you stress. People generally bring about stress since it's in human nature. All relationships have limits. For better or worse, the people in your life will not be there at the end. People come and go like the wind. Don't get caught up in trying to satisfy people who aren't worth it. There should be zero stress in a relationship with anyone who says they support you.

ABOUT THE AUTHOR

This book is derived from the experiences of the author, Joseph, and has no correlation to anyone in particular. These are the views in which he sees himself and the people around him. Though a bit dark in nature, Joe's views come from a place of hopelessness and desertion. Though faced with the challenge of love, everyone around you has a story to tell.

ABOUT THE BOOK

This book is for those who seek perfection in everything they do. Whether or not to succeed is another topic, but the attempt has to be made on such a grand scale that there is no way to fail. When you play video games, after a certain point, you have to gain a high score for recognition. The higher you climb, the bigger the reward. You gain experience and points along the way. This book will show you how to get more points during your journey to success.

www.ingramcontent.com/pod-product-compliance
Lightning Source LLC
LaVergne TN
LVHW041802060526
838201LV00046B/1099